HEME AQUÍ
HERE I AM

My reconciliation with life

Nora Lelczuk Goldfinger

Lelczuk, Nora

Heme aquí Here I Am: my reconciliation with life / Nora Lelczuk Goldfinger

Original Title: Heme aquí : mi reconciliación con la vida / Nora Lelczuk.

ISBN 978-1-7335165-5-6

1. Autobiography.

Copyright@2020Lelczuk-Goldfinger

Translation: Brenda Carol Lelczuk

Cover design: Federico Pallas

©2020 **Goldfinger**

First edition in Spanish ©2018. IMPREX Ediciones Marzo de 2018. Merlo - Bs. As. Argentina. Editorial production and text revision: Rut Beresovsky.

All rights reserved. No part of this publication may be reproduced, distributed, or transmitted in any form or by any means, including photocopying, recording, or other electronic or mechanical methods, without the prior written permission of the author, except in the case of brief quotations embodied in critical reviews and certain other noncommercial uses permitted by copyright law. For permission requests, write to hemeaqui@hemeaqui.org

Heme Aquí, Here I Am: my reconciliation with life

[handwritten dedication:] UN ABRAZO NORA POR TU TRABAJO CON ESTE LIBRO — Roberto de Vicenzo [1]

---

[1] Greetings to Nora on acassion of this book publication by Master Roberto De Vicenzo.

To my daughters:

*Evelyn, Vanina y Melisa,
who are my creative force,
my unconditional support
and the Meaning of my Life.*

TABLE OF CONTENTS

PROLOGUE	1
THE STORY OF MY LIFE	3
HANDICAPPED OR PEOPLE WITH SPECIAL NEEDS?	18
GOLF AND LEARNING	21
SCHOOL AND GROWTH	25
GOLF AS ANALOGY OF LIFE	27
GOLF AND INCLUSION	29
AN IDEA IS BORN: A DETERMINATION IS BORN	32
INCLUSION AND INUSPSIQUIS	36
BASIS OF THE METHODOLOGY HEME AQUÍ	41
EDUCATIONAL GOALS	
SPORT GOALS	
SOCIAL GOALS	
STUDENT GOALS	
GOLDFINGER METHOD PEDAGOGY	43
HEME AQUÍ, HERE I AM FOUNDATIONS	71
EDUCATIONAL LEVEL	71
CREATIVE LEVEL	72
ATTITUDINAL LEVEL	73
TESTIMONIES	74
NORA LELCZUK CV	82

Nora Lelczuk Goldfinger

*My life showed me the path to create this school,
and this school thaught me to say:*

"YES TO LIFE!"

N.L.G.

Heme Aquí, Here I Am: my reconciliation with life

PROLOGUE

Many times have I stared to those images that might lead you to see more than one object, where you can see either two faces or a glass, a face of an old woman or the face of a young lady and many other things. I stare at those pictures bewildered of the unmanageable truth, that what we see, depends on where we focus on.

What I mean is: what do we see when we really focus?

Colleagues from the Gestalt trend have done many researches about these perceptions, and have concluded that what we see as a reality, depends much more on our own reality. Depending on our mood, we might see a face or a glass, and according to our way of life, we might see the old woman or the young woman and so on.

I wonder: what do we see when we see a person with special needs?

Depending on what we focus on, reality would emerge. We could see sadness, sorrow, bitterness, uneasiness, helplessness, or annoyance, but on the other hand, we could see desire of selfimprovement, chances, and opportunities.

Clearly depends on what we focus on, and the true reality would emerge as one thing or another.

What do we see when we see?

Nora and Luis put their focus on the right spot. After becoming parents of a nice young lady with special needs, they focused on what was really important there to see: a daughter.

They also saw a person with talent, with resources and opportunities to self-improvement.

From there on, they had the chance to act accordingly, offering their daughter and many other girls and boys with special needs, the possibility to be seen from a different perspective.

Goldfinger family engaged on this task and moved forward, succeeding to give Vanina a great way of life.

Nora did not settle for anything less on Vanina's wellbeing, that she developed a training method, resulting in a formidable undertaking, which is a very successful Golf School called HERE I AM, "HEME AQUI" that nowadays has headquarters in Argentina and abroad.

School students, young boys and girls with special needs, would play and practice golf to such an extent, as to become instructors of this sport; a sport not easy at all, but, where the physical, emotional, social and spiritual benefits of this practice are clear for all to see.

Nora challenges herself and introduces what they call " the Goldfinger method" which is applied to the golf school nowadays. This method could be easily applied to other artistic, cultural, or sports undertakings too. It is not a mere golf course, but a method of work, which focuses on what a person with special needs, need. The dignity to be considered as a whole, as an integral human being

I consider this introduction of a great public utility for those interested on the subject; it highlights the importance of the human being as a whole, to the point of discovering that the human nature does not accept any disability at all.

I thank Nora and Luis Goldfinger, and to all the boys and girls that took part of the school " Heme Aqui "HERE I AM, and to all those families involved in It. Because they never gave up, or fall for pity, victimization or resentment.

They understood that, there is no living hell that could destroy human dignity; dignity finds its own way of fulfilment. You just have to give permission to yourself.

That is what this book is about.

Claudio García Pintos

THE STORY OF MY LIFE

*Love is the only way to grasp
another human being
in the inner most core of his personality.*

Viktor Frankl

During the ceremony where I received the award, "El sentido de la Vida "(the Meaning of life) I step up and said: When one starts a project one is never alone, there are moments, people and situations, that lead us and show us the right path. That is why I want to share with you who were the ones I relied on, for Vanina to turn into this beautiful lady she is today.

Luis and I were married on March 15th 1981, and after a few days I suffered from spotting, I ran some tests and I realized I was pregnant. I had to rest for few days, and had some kidney stones that really hurt, besides that, everything was normal.

Every month, after each visit to the doctor for my pregnancy and weight examination, I remember that my husband and I went for a coffee, to share our happiness.

Evelyn

January was the scheduled date, when Evelyn was supposed to be born. It is well known that first time mom, always delivers earlier, so by December, I was ready to have my baby, but she was not ready to come out. As January went by with examinations, by February 3rd 6 A.M. my water broke. I had a bath; I called the midwife and went to the clinic. After five hours of labor pains, the baby was not ready to come out. The doctor realized she had the umbilical cord wrapped around her neck. I can still remember how I rushed through the halls on the stretcher, and how afraid I was to fall.

I finally had a Cesarean and a beautiful baby girl was born .Her head was covered in black hair but later, it would turn into golden blond hair. She was the only baby girl born in that clinic, the rest of the babies born that day, were boys.

I was taught to hold her, feed her, and change her diapers.

When thinking about a name for her, my husband and I, came up with the name Evelyn. When my husband said:- Evelyn, tin ,tin and we really loved the musicality in it (and without knowing, we were guiding her through what it would be her destiny in life: dancing, singing and acting)

We named her Evelyn, and her middle name would be Yael, in Hebrew.

Luis and I got married when we were in our thirties, and by the time Evelyn was born, grandsons and nephews in the family were already grown up, so Evelyn was treated like she was the first baby in the family.

She was like a colourful picture, blond with big blue eyes and long eyelashes.

I sanitized the air she breathed, you had to wash your hand in order to hold her and if she was to fall asleep, new clean bed sheets should be put in her cradle every time.

I used to read her a lot, and Luis used to dance with her.

Evelyn was still a baby, when my aunt was reading her a book, and as she turned the page Evelyn said; you haven't read the whole page!

I was living a dream. It felt like I was walking through clouds of cotton.

When I used to go for a walk on the park with her, I felt like a peacock showing off all my colored feathers.

After our winter holidays, my friend Aida suggested taking Evelyn to a kindergarten. And I did, but I can still remember how she cried every time I left her there.

By October, the same year, Luis, Evelyn and I made a trip. Everybody was delighted by my daughter's maturity, how she could talk, her good behaviour and her intelligence.

Therefore, when we got back from our trip, there was no use for taking her back to the kindergarten again, so I decided to take her to work with me, at Luis's furniture store, and she stayed in her cradle like a doll.

When I got pregnant the next time, I started with spotting again, so the doctor ordered an echography and realized I had placenta occlusive, so he advised me not to lift anything heavy and not to make any effort. I took every precaution about that matter, and continued with my happy life with my gorgeous baby girl.

However, I had a feeling. Though I felt very lucky to have Evelyn, I was now concerned because Luis was 46 and I was 35 by the time of my second pregnancy. I asked the doctor to run some tests to see if everything was ok with the baby, but he discouraged us with statistics and data, saying that the probabilities of having a baby with Down syndrome or "mogólico", a stigma label in Spanish that was used at a time, were null. I thought "that would never happen to me, not to us," "that is something that happens to other people," so we moved on and continued with our joyous life.

I was trying to think of a name with the same musicality as when we thought of Evelyn's for our next daughter and I thought about Vanina Noel, but in the Civil Registry, Noel was not allowed to be registered as a name. So in the book of names I found Nahir and I liked it; so we named her Vanina Nahir. Later on, I found out that Nahir, comes from the Hebrew word OR, which means light and brightness.

Vanina

The words mom and dad didn't have the same meaning anymore, they had to be redefined.

Were we going to behave the same way for both daughters?

Were we going to act accordingly?

Were we going to raise both daughters on equal terms?

My ignorance and my bewilderment was so huge when Vanina was born, that I could only think that we have destroyed Evelyn's life. I thought, who would love Evelyn knowing she had a sister with Down syndrome? Will she be able to have friends and boyfriends? This could really be a stigma for Evelyn, I thought.

Picture this: Evelyn was not even two years old, at that time.

Everything was a blur at the beginning I could not see the light; I could only see disappointment, fear, frustration and ignorance, deep ignorance.

Many years later, that deep ignorance, would make me change my decisions and my attitude towards life. That was the exact moment, when I chose to educate through golf.

I thought I would not able to live with Vanina, I thought about giving her on adoption, I wasn't thinking about her as a person, I was thinking about her as something you label: she was "mongol"* and that, made me mentally unstable.

When I went to the neonatal nursery, all the nurses there, were spoiling her, telling me Vanina was cutest one in there. She was blonde and she had a chubby round little face.

I remember a funny story about that day.

My very close friend Aida, came to visit me to the clinic, and the only thing I kept talking about, was a perfume that my husband gave me as a gift, and that I wanted to take it back because I already had one just like it…

I didn't want to take Vanina home, but I also didn't want to give her in adoption or take her to an institution.

My family owned a property in Santa Fe province, with a big house and land where I used to go frequently to ride horses and enjoy nature. It was a place where it felt like home. A couple lived there as householders of the property, with whom we had a very good relationship. Mrs. Maidana took care of her children, others who were adopted, and also of any soul in need of care. She took care of all with great love. So I thought about her to take care of Vanina. I knew she was going to love her and take good care of her.

So I entrusted Vanina to my uncle and aunt, Chuche and Eugenia, to take her there.

Meanwhile I was locked down at home with the blinds shut, crying all day.

I cannot even remember who took care of Evelyn those days.

My grandfather, my dear grandpa Aron, who lived in the province of Entre Rios, passed away during those days and I couldn't go there because I just had the cesarean operation.

I didn't want to see anybody except my brother Jorge and my sister Eva, they were there for me, all the time.

I was suggested to go to a therapy treatment, together with

Luis, and so we went. First meeting was ok, but the second time, the doctor didn't show up; we were just told that there was a confusion regarding the date.

Can you imagine? All that we were going through and the doctor didn't show up?

Evelyn's paediatrician, Dr. Cukier, had no experience about this situation either, but he did what he could, to help us, and introduced us to a family that had a daughter like Vanina.

I called that family to arrange a meeting, and the girl's mom on the phone said: if Vanina is like Lía, you are going to be ok. So I prayed that she was. That family were the Zvetelman's. We went to their house, and while on the elevator, Roberto said: so you have a daughter with Down syndrome right? Suddenly something inside of me, clicked. Vanina wasn't mongol, she was a girl with Down syndrome .Those words change my whole vision, she suddenly became a person, not something or someone with a label.

I think it was in that moment, in the elevator, when I took control of my own life back again.

It's funny to think that many years after that, I would be like a guide for Lía in many ways.

I decided I was overthinking about the situation, may be too much, and it was time to get in touch with my feelings. Next month Luis and I headed to Santa Fe to look for Vanina.

This was the scenario: our house in Santa Fe was merely 50 meters away from Mrs. Maidana's house. I was in the main house but Vanina was with " Mrs. Maidana". I asked her husband, to tell her, to give me the baby back, but she refused.

I wanted to give the baby bottle to Vanina, and "Mrs. Maidana" wanted to feed her too. It was a funny situation, like two lionesses fighting over their cub, but me, I was ready to be Vanina's mother.

Next month, Vanina and I went to Entre Rios, to my uncle's, Tito and Adela. My parents went with me, and Luis came and went again and again.

During those two months we stayed in Entre Rios, Vani and I began to know each other.

Back in Buenos Aires, every time we visited the paediatrician,

I kept asking him: will she be able to walk? Will she be able to speak? Will she be able to reach and hand me over her shoes? Will she understand?

Vanina started her therapy treatment at Dr. Castaño's clinic, beginning with her motor skills treatment and speech therapy twice a week and we continued with the excercises at home.

Vani was born in November and by next July, I had a surgery, because I had a nodule in the thyroid gland. After that, Luis promised himself that if everything went ok, we were going to take a comforting trip; Evelyn, and the two of us. My sisters in law, Bety, Luis's sister and Susy, Jorge's wife would take care of Vanina while we were away. They took good care of Vanina, taking her to early stimulation training and the neurologist twice a week. Thank you both!

When Vanina was two, she began a therapeutic kindergarten at the Castaño's clinic, but when she turned four, I started to look for a kindergarten with an inclusion project.

I went to too many meetings, in different kindergartens, with many different Principals, some of them made me wait and wouldn't meet with me. Or if they did meet with me they would give all kinds of excuses not accept Vanina. Some told me that if they accepted my daughter, other parents would take their children away from the school, and that the school would not be able to face that economic challenge. They treated us in such a way, that made us feel like we had some contagious disease.

Sometimes I was in such a stress and anger that made me go voiceless.

However, I met Alan Leon's parents, Alan was a boy with Down syndrome too, and they talked to me about a kindergarten where they considered social inclusion.

That Kindergarten was called "Amanecer", which means sunrise, and it really felt like a sunrise to me.

Later I met Tati, a wonderful person. She was the Principal of Oaky Kindergarten, where they believed in inclusion too. There, Vanina went until she was 11, due to the fact that I couldn't find another school for her with the same characteristics.

I didn't want Vani to fall behind with her education, so Tati suggested for Vani to take private classes at home, in the morning, with a teacher called Rosita. While in the afternoons, Vani would continue taking classes of music, tennis, English and theatre at the kindergarten. Vani still remembers how much she learned in the English classes at Oaky kindergarten.

Melisa

When Melisa was born, it felt like making peace with life.

Vani was two years and two months old when Melisa was born; and they were practically raised as twins, since they were going through the same stages of development at the same time.

Melisa was like a guide to Vanina, and she was always there to protect her.

They would fight and play and share good times together, just like any other sisters.

Even nowadays Vani would only listen to Melisa's advice, unconditionally. When we don't know how to handle a matter with Vani, we would ask Melisa to mediate.

The growing process of both girls was similar, until they reached the pre- adolescence stage.

Meli's growth was geometric, while Vani's growth was arithmetic.

Meli had many subjects of interest, which she developed quickly.

She went to parties and went out with her friends with no problem, but for Vanina, it was a completely different story.

Even though I always believed in inclusion, I realized that, no one fits everywhere, with everybody, all the time. That was the reason why, the group of people Vani belonged to, in her school, was so important.

Evelyn and Melisa were two of the biggest motivations Vanina had at hand.

Meli is joyous, funny, smart, enjoyable, pleasant and very active.

Evelyn is a natural born artist; she is creative, she is a thinker and a challenging person.

Therefore, Vanina learned everything about acting and singing, from, Evelyn's world.

Both sisters have a great influence on Vani. Whenever I have an important decision to make about Vanina, or about life, I turn to them for advice.

All of us in our family like to dance, sing, write, and read, and we discuss everything together. Vanina, like the rest of us, has her arguments and we always listen to her. Sometimes she surprises us with her clear and deep thoughts.

We are five in the family, and we do everything together. This is Luis' motto: Inclusion starts at home.

This story would not be complete if I don't talk about a very important part of our life.

Shabbat

Shabbat is a day of worship and rest, which begins with the sunset every Friday, until the rise of stars on Saturday night.

When Vani was three years old, we used to meet every Friday, with other families for Shabbat, taking turns to go to each other's house. We were around seventeen people altogether.

Every Friday we went to the temple and afterwards, we would meet in our home, dressing our table with the best cutlery and tablecloths, to celebrate Shabbat with our friends.

We said the blessings, we sang, we ate, and enjoyed being together as a big family. It was a time of joy and noise, and love, respect for each other, and honesty.

Kids talked, played, and laughed all together. And there was Vani, just like any other, surrounded by love. It was a great stimulus for her too.

Those meetings took place along 20 years, until one of our friends went to live abroad. But those moments, and the images of our strong relationship, the lessons learned together, would never fade because they were vast.

We still meet with Leo and Claudia's family on Shabbat.

School Inclusion

The learning experience in Oaky kindergarten was exhausted, so I needed a new school for Vanina, which was not an easy task to do. Not many schools believed in inclusion by that time.

Then, I heard about "Instituto Tognoni" a school that had an interesting inclusion project, but it was a church depending school and I wanted a secular one. Nevertheless, I was introduced to the coordinator of that project in that school, Cristina Lobosco, and we talked a lot about it.

Later on, Elsa Bianchi, Principal of the school, joined us, and I discovered a person with a great sense of education, responsibility and love for others; she was the one that helped developed the project.

Years later, I run into Elsa and she tells me a story.

Vanina and a group of students went on a trip with Elsa, they were on Florida street, talking about geography, when suddenly a woman that was passing by and was listening, approaches Elsa and asks: Why do you bother to teach her all those things?

Vanina answers: so I could talk to people like you!

The parallel integration project would be developed as follows: a group of students with special needs, would work simultaneously with common students.

Common students would keep their corresponding schedule as it is, but they would share activities with students with Down syndrome, like, music, recreational activities, fine arts, lunchtime, campings, or going out.

I think this, was the most important thing to consider, people with special needs, needed a group of belonging, that would improve self-esteem, and from there on, they will be able to show society their skills and improvements achieved.

This would be exactly the same basic outline I would adopt in my golf school later on.

Here I am "Heme Aquí"

During the same period, I came across Martina Samuels, who had a Degree in Education, and together, we tried to introduce this project of integration, to elementary schools of the Jewish community.

Elsa and Cristina joined us and were very supportive about it. They accompanied us to talk about their experiences, to many schools, but we never managed to develop the project.

Cristina insisted on enrolling Vanina in the "Instituto Tognoni".

I call for a family reunion, and Evelyn and Melisa said that, if I considered that, that school was the best choice for Vanina, then I should go ahead and do it…

Elsa on the other hand, didn't have any problem at all to include people of a different religion, to this Catholic school. Good for her!!

And that was how Vanina, went to "Insituto Tognoni de la Sagrada Eucaristía" in Palermo.

Bat Mitzvah

I want to tell a story that perfectly describes Vanina as a whole.

At the age of 12, young Jewish girls, make a commitment to become part of the Jewish people in a ceremony called Bat Mitzva. They study the holy verses for a year to be prepared for that ceremony.

We were on our way back from Evelyn's Bat Mitzva ceremony, in our car, when suddenly I hear Vanina's voice from behind my seat asking: Mom: when do I get to celebrate my bat mitzvah?

I was in shock, and trying to act normal, I answered: you will celebrate your Bat Mitzva of course, but when it comes your time.

So I went to ask rabbis Dani Goldman and Mario Rojzman, from Bet El community ,if Vanina could celebrate her Bat Miztva, and they said: Sure, Why not?

Laura Laufer, a sweet young lady, with a remarkable inner strength and joy, was Vanina's teacher twice a week, to teach her all there is to know about Bat Mitzva's ceremony. They took it very serious!

So the time for her Bat Mitzva's came, it was a Saturday, October 13° th 1996, 9:30 A.M in Bet El Temple. We were so nervous!

Vanina received a blessing from the Rabbis, and we gifted her a pair of chandeliers.

Paula and Vani were sitting on the stairs underneath the Holy Ark and the ceremony began.

Guided by Paula, Vani started to tell the part of the bible of that week, she was confident, and the easiness with which she did it marvelled everybody.

Even today, people that were at the ceremony tells me how wonderful she was.

What I want to stand out here, is that Vani herself, decided to make that commitment, with such a conviction, reassurance and decision that left us all marvelled.

Our gift for her, was to play the play Beauty and the Beast, which she loved so much. We wore all the real costumes of the play.

Actors, choreographers, writers and producers were: her sisters, her aunt Eva and her cousin Maxi . Luis, her dad, played the role of the beast, and Vani of course played the Beauty.

For Melisa's Bat mitzvah, Evelyn sang the tango "El dia que me quieras" to her, a tango that Evelyn recorded with Alberto, Berbara, who made the musical arrangements of the songs of Heme Aqui School of Golf. After Evelyn's song, Vanina spontaneously started to sing the same song in front of everybody, a cappella! People could not believe their eyes and ears!

I made the invitations for Vanina's ceremony myself. The Statue of Liberty and Vanina's face were printed on them; in order to show her freedom of choice and her responsibility for her search of meaning.

The word Hineni was the one chosen to give the whole thing a meaning, which stands for HERE I AM ,"Heme aqui". Because she chose to belong to the Jewish people.

Later, HEME AQUI, would be the name I choose for the First Golf School for People with special Needs, which I found in June 1999 with a methodology I will develop along in this book.

This school is of a great importance in our family. My husband, my three daughters and I are completely involved in this work, bringing us together even closer as a family.

People who contributed in Vanina's life.

I met Eugenio Perez Soto, who was a psychologist, and with whom Evelyn was taking therapy sessions with. He was also the founder of the Centre of existential psychology and Logotherapy, everything I know about Logotherapy I learned it from him. That therapy would help me create and found the Golf School, once overcame ignorance and pain.

In 1994, Evelyn went to Chile with Bet El community. While at Ezeiza airport, waiting for our children to come back, I met Dr Benenzon. He was a father waiting for his daughter too, but he was also a music therapist. He asked me if I was willing to write my experience with Vanina, in a book he was writing, which talked about the life of young people with special needs and their parents.

I accepted of course and my story was developed in that book called: "Los Discapacitados y Nosotros" Disabled people and Us.

Dr Benenzon was the one who showed me to walk through the path of disabled people process, and he encouraged me to introduce my work called:" Integration is a way of living" at a congress in 1998 at the Catholic University of Rome.

Wain family kindly printed the poster I designed and presented at the congress.

Our cousin Masha in Florida, USA, let us stayed over her house during our holidays many times. She was always so kind and loving; she used to encourage me with the golf school. Our talks were very rewarding, and she loved to give me family advices too. Once she said, with her Venezuelan accent: Hey girl! You should write a book!

Vacationing there, allowed us to visit David's Leadbetter golf school, where Vanina and I received training.

Marta is my faithful housekeeper, always taking good care of

Vanina, giving her the best of times, as if she was her own daughter.

My family supported us at all times, giving Vanina all the love she needed.

Cousin Papchu would take the girls out to eat and go for a ride every week.

Vani was in love with her cousin Maxi, he was the one that played the role of Gastón in Beauty and The Beast play. She would call Maxi six or seven times a day, she loved talking on the phone until one in the morning with him. Her crush for him faded later, but she still calls him from time to time.

I want to thank my friends Leo and Claudia for their support; they always included Vanina in their activities, meetings, parties and trips we shared.

Grandparents and Aunt

Grandma *Bobe* Aída used to cook special meals for Vanina like latkes, Spanish tortilla, spinach and cheese quiche, pletzalach and many more sweet things, when she stayed over for the weekends. She would also tell stories about when she was young and sang Polish songs for her. Vanina misses her songs and her loving care.

Grandpa *Zeide* Pedro, used to play hide and seek with Vanina all around the house, they would share summers together in Punta del Este beach. Vanina had such a long hair that she would like to play with it and put it over her grandpa's head as a wig.

With Grandma, *Bobe* Chola, had a relationship based on conversations, every day, they would talk about school, friends, boyfriends, and her activities. They liked to play rummy, going out to eat, and spend summers together too.

Aunt Evita deserves a completely new chapter.

She is called "THE aunt" or "Tweety."

She is like her very own confessor; she is the one that Vanina turns to, whenever there is something wrong, when she gets angry at us, or when she has big news.

Vanina loves to spend time with her, Evita is her paint

teacher too and they also like to play rummy.

Who is Vanina today?

She is a young independent self-assured person, who enjoys life and her activities.

She reads and writes with not so many errors, she has some skills on information technology. She can do some work around the house. She can run errands, like going to the groceries store. She plays golf, she can ride horses, enjoys going out with her friends, she likes singing, and she is an excellent actress, and she likes to write poems and recite them too.

Whenever we travel, she shows her passport in such an easy and confident way, worth admiring. Many times she travelled abroad by herself.

Vanina Worked for the ORT school library for more than 17 years.

She now works as a Junior Sport Leader, training others on the Goldfinger Method in the Golf school "Heme Aqui". She is the one that talks on interviews for the media; and she is the one that explains how the methodology works. She is the one that introduces the School in a meeting, the one that trains teachers, and who talks about the meaning of inclusion in golf.

Vanina is very well known for giving speeches in any occasion, religious celebrations, family meetings or national holidays. She always has something to say. She is confident, she likes to shows her feelings and feels comfortable giving speeches. She is really theatrical, delicate and fond of welcoming people. She is in love with life; she is an example for all of us.

Thanks to Vani we have met a lot of people, we carried out activities, we went to conventions, talks, contests, we were interviewed, and we founded The school of Life, which rewarded us as a family, and as human beings.

Vani is an important part of the Golf School, she is the one that shows swing movement to the students, the one who helps in class and enjoys being with all the students, but as a family, we all contribute with the proper working order of The School.

Evelyn is the educational Leader of The School, apart from writing and directing musical plays for children, she writes and sings the songs of our methodology.

Melisa is the coordinator of The School; she takes part on the designing of the methodology, works with the youngsters, and has an excellent relationship with them.

Luis takes care of the public relations of The School and is the photographer too.

And me, I can say, as a mother, that I went through an inside process of change, having faced the inexorable realities that life presented, which helped me to discover through suffering, as Viktor Frankl calls it, the real Meaning of Life.

HANDICAPPED OR PEOPLE WITH SPECIAL NEEDS?

Persons with disabilities include those who have long-term physical, mental, intellectual or sensory impairments, which in interaction with various barriers may hinder their full and effective participation in society on an equal basis with others
     Convention on the Rights of Persons with Disabilities
          Law N°26378 Article 1 section 2

Part of my anguish when Vani was born, was because I thought of her in terms of abilities, I didn't think of her as a person. I missed the fact that she had a name, that we had given her. ,I was missing the fact that she had her vey own life. She was the one that had the greatness to include us as a family making us better persons.

People did not know how to call those persons that were different from "normal".

After going through many different names such as: mentally handicapped, retarded, idiot, mongol, by the year 2006, at the Convention on the Rights of Persons with Disabilities, the term persons with disabilities was established. Even so, I always refused to use the term disability, beacause I think it refers to something you cannot accomplish, something you cannot make or feel. That definition takes away all the chances right from the beginning.

I was once in a convention in Mar del Plata, and a speaker was lecturing about the Convention of People with Disabilities, when suddenly a very well prepared young, active, working lady stood up and said: enough! I'm tired of being called disabled! I don't want to be labelled! I have a name and I want to be called by it .And she sat down very angry.

Although the speaker lady felt really uncomfortable, because she had to continue with the subject, I started to applaud that young lady, because I knew how she felt.

Once I was a speaker at the Professional Council of Economic Science, talking about The Golf School, and   I exposed about the deep loneliness people with disabilities feel, (I decided to use this term since everybody uses it) when María Elis, a student of the School, stood up and said: Nora you are wrong, I'm not a person with disabilities, I'm like any other person, I don't want to be called like that!

Silence invaded the room, and I replied to her very calm, I agree with you María Elis, I don't like it either.

I do understand that, from the legal and universal point of view, we have to adopt common terms, in order to know what we are talking about, when as to laws, self-independence, life rights, right to your own choices and right to education refers.

Since I founded The School I always use the term people with special needs, Why?

Because I think that I'm talking about people first. I don't think about their abilities, I think of them as persons, and from there on, I treat them as equals and add it to my world.

Only then, I Talk about the special needs.

Society is only prepared for "normal", normal health, normal odontology, normal psychology, and normal laws. But our youngsters are not normal for this society.

Many professionals have never had the chance to relate in any way with people with special needs at all. That is the reason why, I say they have special needs, in terms of education, medical care, sexual concerns, dental treatments, or in terms of love and being loved. They have their own special needs, and there is an urge to fulfil and answer those needs.

There are many communities that due to their education, their culture or war history, deal everyday with persons with different disabilities, and society itself takes responsibility of fulfilling those needs. Such as: infrastructure, educational opportunities provided by the government, working laws that include them in the open market, or health care laws covering their needs by the time they are adults.

Nowadays, due to the efforts made by parents, teachers, educators and sport figures, we are breaking rigid structures of thought, and we are opening minds towards people with special needs. Society is becoming aware of the potential of people with special needs have, to develop themselves and being part of the community.

If we want this process of inclusion to succeed, society must be ready to make changes in many areas.

Albert Einstein once said:" it is easier to disintegrate an atom than a prejudice"

Inclusion and diversity are two sides of the same coin .If there is no diversity, what do I want to include? Others or myself? What is the criteria I will use? I am the variable.

If I'm to include, I have to accept others as they are, not only for what I think they are, but because of what they are valuable for.

We build stereotypes in our minds, and that is how we visualize and see the world. But there is a part of the whole that is missing to understand others.

Others see me, as their own imaginary stereotype. But what happens if I'm the different one, and is the other one that does not include Me? That changes everything, I'm the one that wants to be part of, and the other one will consider if he wants to accept me or not. This is very common in small towns with close or traditional societies. Where the odd one out is the one that threatens their own survival or historic continuity. How do I feel when this happens?

What is the criteria I use for diversity?

Stephen Covey says: we should be reminded that diversity is not something external but internal"

Diversity is the colour of my eyes, my hair, my race, my religion my political ideas, but acceptance of diversity of thought, wishes, attitudes, convictions, feelings, dreams, or beliefs, is where the challenge lies.

A passage from Pirkei Avot (ethical book of our Fathers) says: I have to love others for what he is, not for I think he is valuable for. If that were the case, we would accomplish better relationships with others by recognizing the person he really is, and not the image we have in our minds, according to our expectations.

We all fell in love once, to find out later he was not what we expected. Right? Of course he wasn't, because we see others the way we want them to be, we don't take the time to see him as he really is, because it would be harder to accept him in our world.

We are not accepting diversity once again.

By accepting or rejecting diversity, we have the opportunity to choose.

How can I be part of the criteria?

The criteria I use would always be someone like me. We don't do it consciously, it is just the way we see the world, and we act and think accordingly. So, if I stop labelling people as taller, bigger, or different than me, there is a chance to incorporate others in my mind, in my body and in my spirit. That is the moment, when real acceptance and inclusion takes place.

GOLF AND LEARNING

Inclusion means that we can be together sharing activities, with everyone's individuality taken into account, opening to others, learning to respect everybody's limitations and appreciating others' possibilities.

Following these guidelines is that we thought about golf as a sport. Golf teaches us the real meaning of this generous and sensitive word that is handicap.

Handicap means, a mutual advantage given to the competitors to equal the possibilities of winning.

Handicap is a beautiful word, so difficult to consider nowadays, but is also one of the rules and conditions to play this singular sport.

Golf respects diversity and the different abilities of all, giving the same opportunities to all.

In This competitive society, winning is a privilege of a few.

But this activity is a conceivable dream for everybody, without exclusions, no rejections and with the premise: love your fellow men like you love yourself.

The School of Life "Heme Aqui" Here I AM, works with people with Down Syndrome, persons without a diagnose, persons with mental disabilities, autism, or with Asperger. Every pathology has its own physical characteristics, but they also have something in common, which is the chance to learn with an appropriate education. And from there on, they will have the possibility to have fun, try to achieve their goals and fulfil them.

It is very well known that stimulation is a priority for children with special needs.

Carlos Gianantonio used to say: "stimulation should have started yesterday"

Stimulation is the most important thing for all the kids, and even more for people with disabilities, concerning that their learning is slower.

They need to be guided in their learning process, because they need to learn, what other kids learn instinctively.

That is the reason why we developed a new and different methodology of teaching. Based on the methodology of learning, the using of colors, the use of games as a strategy, by applying down to earth mathematics, and implementing new ways of teaching social studies, in order to capitalize their abilities.

Their attention is weak, and they get tired easily, so we have to explore new ways of keeping their attention.

Their learning process is slow, so we have to work with repetitions; because although they say they comprehend, there is a need to reinforce what was learned.

The learning process should be developed in phases, with repetitions, and move to the next level of complexity slowly.

People with Down Syndrome have difficulties in their oral language, and sometimes they are not able to answer in an oral way, questions or instructions. It's difficult for them to read and write, because their pronunciation is not correct, making it hard to write the words with the same letters. Those who can achieve good verbal skills are able to accomplish better reading and writing abilities.

We have to consider that, for people with special needs, expression is more important than comprehension; that is the reason they can understand more than they can express. We have to be prepared to communicate in many ways. Paying attention to their body, their hands, their gestures, and sounds.

Another obstacle people with special needs have to

overcome, is their fine and gross motor skills.

Fine motor skills, like performing the players it's a sign of motor complexity, and, to what golf concerns, you have to work a lot with the way you put your hand and fingers on the grip. About gross motor skills, difficulties appear when we have to deal with rotation movements, muscle tone, position of the legs and movements of the arms.

The shape of their hands are different from one another too. Some has shorter fingers and some has their fingers closer to one another, some has the palm of their hand shorter, making it difficult for them to handle the grip due to their lack of elasticity.

We have to work on the instructions given and their comprehension, their physical difficulties to handle the grip, the stance, and the swing, according to the possibilities of everyone.

Two levels of learning have to be combined and joined at the same time: cognitive and physical.

Instructions on the usage of every element, the stance and the swing, have to be attractive, comprehensive, and easy to learn .We also adapt the performance of their movements to their possibilities.

The traditional way of teaching golf is, teachers show their students how to hit with the different clubs and the best way to perform the shots, and they practice.

Many golf terms have to be remembered, like: grip, stance, hand positions, turns, backswing, downswing, finish. The student has to comprehend and process all that information given, in order to hit the ball correctly.

In the specific case of our school, is essential to work with the instructors previously. Training them to explain every movement many times, for the students to comprehend. A movement has to be taught in two or three phases for the students to fully incorporate it.

Repetition contributes to obtain good results, turning them into qualified golfers, to go out in the golf course and play the game.

In order to make changes on people with special needs, In "Heme Aqui" Here I Am, we focus on different fields, pedagogical, psychological and the athletic area, so they can achieve their goals in their uniqueness.

SCHOOL AND GROWTH

It is this spiritual freedom – which cannot be taken away – that makes life purposeful and meaningful.
Viktor Frankl

His own image and likeness
In the beginning "...You will be like Gods"
I'm expecting a son of His own Image and Likeness.
We tend to think that, that image we have in our minds physically and mentally, reflects what we are.
How is that image? We want our children to be like us,because of our own narcissism, the more like us the better.
When a baby with special needs is born, our world crumbles.
Many questions with no answers begin to invade our minds. Why me? What am I going to do? What is going to happen to my family, to my other kids?
We tend to overthink situations and we forget to feel. We don't realize that what was born, was a human being. We are ready to be mothers and fathers of normal people, with a normal family according to role models and standards, and that, is the way we want our family to be.
Any variance of that normality causes us fear, because it compels us to question ourselves as persons, our principles, and we have to rephrase the words mom and dad.
Am I the mother of a child with special needs? Do I have to be the same person or should I change? Am I the same mother for one son that for the other? The real question is, Who is The Other?
That was the time where my ignorance and doubts appeared. Would I be the mother this child needs? Will I be able to give him all he needs? How Am I going to fit in with my standard family? How will the society respond? I doubt myself and I doubt my marriage.
First my reasoning tells me what and how I should feel, I overthink the situation, but my feelings are paralyzed. I feel what the reason tells me to feel, and then, I try to picture my life

from now to the rest of my days, with this daughter, so different, but wanted.

I torture myself with questions. Will she understand me? Will she be able to walk? Is she going to be like a plant? What school will I send her? Will she be accepted? What will the boyfriends of my other daughters think? But I keep thinking, eventhough, I know my daughter are still babies.

Will she be doomed to a life with no laughter or expectations? Or will she be able to enjoy life?

But one day, I woke up resolved to feel and stop questioning me. I began to feel her. I began to look at her as a human being, to realize she was hungry, and sleepy, cold, and hot too, just like anybody else

I see her laughing and it amazes me, she is not a shadow, she is my fellowship. I realize she was created by God's image and likeness.

I realized that the image and likeness is neither physical nor intellectual, there was another dimension that I didn't take into account, the spiritual one.

There are many kinds of demands and needs in which we are alike, love, feelings, creativity, dreams, joy, sincerity…

As Rabbi Goldman says:" they look more than God than we do, because they have so much love inside of them, and God is love"

Therefore, I begun to feel and I started to discover and find us, as human beings.

Human beings created as image and likeness, able to constitute a family, just like that, a family with no labels, no fix schemes, and together, we begin to walk through a path full of ups and downs but as we walk, we learn.

GOLF AS ANALOGY OF LIFE

Let's think about golf as an analogy of life.

The tee stroke is our birth, as when we enter life for the first time. If we are lucky enough a caddie or an assistant will guide us, and correct us, reminding us and advising us how to make that first shot.

This guide will help me with my posture, my way of handling the grip, and will show me where to aim, never to lose sight, to focus towards a life I will shape along each shot.

Nothing is for sure; sometimes the wind or anxiety will play against us, and before we realize, we are out of bounds. It requires a great effort to focus again, I have to pay attention and focus on my target, the green and the hole.

As if I wasn't distracted and confused enough, the green as in life, displays obstacles. Showing me this attractive blue lake and golden sands that catches my eyes, distracting me, taking me to a place I shouldn't be, leaving me behind in the game.

Places I just have to get out of, because they are only obstacles.

This is one of the most important and crucial moments: I can chose between being defeated by these external obstacles or decide to move on, and take those problems as a real opportunity to learn and grow, to overcome them. Eventhough It might take many shots until I can make the right movement, if I keep in mind what I have learned, I know that accepting the challenge, is the first step to move forward.

When I find the green again, I will feel like it's my place, the space where I can accomplish my goals that seemed so far away before. It's a time to enjoy and consider every move, feeling the sweet taste of the next victory. Ignoring for a moment all the struggles, I make the last shot and if I make it to the hole, I have accomplished my goal. And when I see the ball flying, time stops, and I'm the owner of my dreams.

"Heme Aqui" has succeed.

I won a battle, I played my game, and the next hole is waiting for me.

I feel confident but I begin all over again.

Every hole is a game in itself, a new phase in life; I have to move on, I should move forward in my new projects and opportunities to grow. I have to keep playing golf as in life.

I repeat: there are internal and external barriers. The Internal are the ones I have already began to modify, but the external ones are still not in order.

I have accepted my daughter and I want to give her the best, just like to my other daughters. I can see that I have done a lot. But there is still ignorance, and fear, and lack of opportunities in the society, which makes me work even harder for her to be accepted.

I seek opportunities; I look for schools, jobs, and sports to include her. Moreover, I chose golf because of the possibilities I knew it would offer, which is Inclusion .But I encounter a different reality.

Persons with disabilities cannot play golf. I was told!

When I introduced my project to many professionals, they said: "they won't be able to play, they don't understand"

I realized that they had no idea at all about that matter, because they never had the chance to see them playing.

Many years later, they would became real enthusiasts of our students, encouraging them, by inviting them to play, teaching them, enjoying their company and cherishing their goals.

Noone would have thought that people with special needs could play golf; it was not considered a game apt for them. This was the first obstacle I encounter when facing society. They thought people with special needs were not apt to play golf.

I had to make a decision: I either accepted this reality or dealt with it.

How do I deal with it? Will it be worth it? What would the results be? Once I decided it would be worth it, I didn't know how to carry it on. What are the possibilities of succeeding? What is the purpose of teaching golf? What is the merit of this new activity? What is it good for? Can I turn it into something positive?

GOLF AND INCLUSION

Heme Aqui was mold and founded on a concept based on the biopsychic social and spiritual idea. With an inclusive perspective to work with the students.

From the biological point of view, we stimulate concentration; we work on the physical structure, improving coordination, posture and the body image.

From the psyche point of view, we work with self-esteem, encouraging personal development and their sense of belonging.

Taking into account that each individual cannot function without the ethic-spiritual part, we focused on team spirit, friendship, respect and sincerity.

Each student is considered as a whole, acting in the complex universe of the human world, showing their uniqueness to the society, to be admitted as a fellowship with their own particularities and universalities.

We work every day to show society that they can .They can play golf among equals and among other people. This is what we called inclusion, the real meaning of the word and of our school.

From the social point of view, we encourage to strengthen their sense of group, to be involve, to play with games specially designed for the students, and to share their experiences with the rest.

This helped us to create a sense of belonging, because they found a group of friends to celebrate their birthdays and parties and share going out into the society, together.

As a school we have grown and bloomed, we are being recognized and respected. We began to play inclusive tournaments. Giving way to their self-confidence, demonstrating that they measure up to the demands of this sport.

They develop their skills creating possibilities as a result of their training.

Even tough they may have a body with certain disadvantages, it is no obstacle to self-improvement, and they adapt themselves to make a good swing, because they have the desire to succeed.

When we refer to the physical and spiritual barriers they need to overcome, they do it in a creative way.

It is said that people with mental disabilities are not able to create, but they are showing they can.

Viktor Frankl, founder of Logotherapy, calls this, willingness of sense.

Willingness focused on the predisposition of a person to change reality into possibilities, through attainable actions. Willingness to accept and fulfil a mission having been confronted to.

Willingness motivates, and makes people free to play golf to be included into society, let alone being a person with special needs.

As to what self-esteem concerns, all the benefits obtained are reassured. They are sure of their accomplishments, they like what they do, and with whom, because they found new friends and they meet new people to relate to.

They enjoy playing a sport that gives a new perspective to their family, parents, brothers and sisters.

Heme Aqui methodology proposal is, that all the students should receive a trophy, because we don't evaluate their sport abilities, but their intention, dedication and accomplishments, because our objective, is to encourage their confidence.

Students like to talk about their accomplishments at the dinner table too, with parents and sisters just like everybody else. We advise them to they keep a special place in the house where to put their trophies, newspaper cut-outs, magazines, and all the material handed out in the school to have their very own golf little corner.

During a very difficult stage as the adolescence is, when they finish school, young people with special needs begin to feel lonely, they don't see their school friends anymore and find themselves with no group where to belong to.

School of life "Heme Aqui, Here I Am", gives the opportunity to share a sport, meetings, birthdays, family situations, a place to talk about their needs, and to socialize. They are happy to attend because they know they will find their friends there, and together they would overcome their differences.

A place where to feel confident as to declare: YES TO LIFE AND YES TO THE MEANING OF LIFE.

AN IDEA IS BORN:
A DETERMINATION IS BORN

The search for meaning in a man's life constitutes a primary force and not a secondary rationalization of their instinctive impulses.

Viktor Frankl

Ever since Vani was born, I worked in favour of the Inclusion, which is a two way path: The ones that realize the effort people with special need make to attain their goals, and the ones that coexist and receive stimulation in a natural way and get ready to live inside the society.

From the sport point of view, I wondered what sports Vanina could practise with other youngsters as an equal. I knew it would be impossible to include her in team sports like volley ball or handball because of the dynamic of the game. So I enrol her in gymnastics, where she did obtain a trophy once, and she also tried swimming, but they were all individual sports, that, even though she was with other common kids, she wouldn't establish any real relationship.

When she started to play tennis, I realized that her mates were also people with special needs.

That was the moment I thought about golf.

Why Golf?

Because I like it, because I've been playing golf for the last 40 years, and when I'm not playing it, I' m talking about it, or visiting golf courses or taking classes. Somewhat, golf was always present in my life. My daughters used to come with me to the golf course, accompanying me and sometimes even try to play.

I noticed that Vanina, besides making good strokes, she answered favourably to that stimulus.

By that time, we made a trip to the United States, with Vani and some friend of ours, Mike and Harriet. We went to play to a very nice small court of 9 holes par-3, with a small lake at the centre, which required precise shots.

Vani surprised us there; her strokes were great with a great score, which lead me to think of golf as the right sport for inclusion.

That was how the project of teaching golf to people with special needs was born.

My daughter was my sense of will. By looking at her, I saw many other young people that could have the same response she had.

Without thinking about it too much, I felt attracted by the idea,I was determined , and I embraced it to make it work. Without even noticing I was uncovering my own mission in life. Thanks Vani for that!

What did I find in golf?

In Golf, the scores are given by the green, allowing people with different abilities to play the same game without changing the individual's game.

Handicap is a term already included in golf's rules, which determines the comparative advantage given to those who know less.

Even normal people born with all the senses and abilities intact, are privileged with handicap to face everyday life.

Handicap means: giving an advantage to those who just started to play the game, the lesser the knowledge of the game, the greater the handicap.

That is another reason that made me think of this sport for inclusion, because it respects the diversity of the different abilities and equals opportunities.

Golf is a game of multiple diversities sharing the same course.

We can extrapolate this sport to another context. Society is build and based on differences. The possibility of inclusion that golf allows, should exist inside the society. I should include You, with your uniqueness, and I should see myself reflected on others, even when the other has a different game level.

Sharing many hours on the course encourages players to begin a relationship, by talking, making comments and advices. The most important thing of all is that, the other players are not my rivals, which helps building a team spirit, because we never know who is going to win out of all the players playing in the course. There is no adversary in front of me; there is no stressing situation with my opponent playing right next to me .I play with another, not against another. Enabling situations where other players can help me, for example, to look for a lost ball, or celebrate a good shot.

As people with special needs grow, their possibilities to be a part of the society are scarcer. Most of them begin a workshop, because the possibilities of their incorporation on the open working market are reduced.

Golf allows them even for a few hours to receive stimulus from normal society. This mutual knowledge works as a mind changer; and when people with special needs play golf with normal people, as they walk through the course, they begin to know each other, having the opportunity to show improvements made with effort but also with joy.

Common people start the game thinking that they are playing with a person with disabilities, but ends up finding out a person, with feelings just like them. Discovering the person behind disabilities. This enables common people to open the working market for people with special needs, including them in institutions, organizations, factories and also including them in their homes and schools.

Through integrated tournaments, people with special needs, work on their Mission, which is to make a more fair and supportive society, where You get closer to Me, through positive determinations. Acknowledging their abilities, their love, their honourable behaviour, their strength and their accomplishments, attained with naivety. Naivety that comes from their inner strength to overcome obstacles.

Let's not forget that people with special needs are conscious of their uniqueness, and that they are being observed, denied, and put to test to attained their objectives. .But nevertheless this emotional burden, duly worked on, blooms in every area where an opportunity is offered.

Distinctive features of golf

It is a sport that strengthens arms and legs; stimulates heart rate; develops concentration; improves body rotation, improves the neuro-muscle coordination; improves posture; increases the ability of vision-motor-space notion; establishes the notion of strength, space and speed; eliminates stress; it is practiced outdoors, surrounded by open green spaces, emphasising the sense of freedom; and golf teaches moral and ethical rules which can be applied on everyday life too.

Why the name "Heme Aqui" Here I AM?

The School of Life **Heme Aqui** Here I Am is based on a philosophy deeply thought of.

How I chose the name.

The school was not named after a sport institution, nor the name of a sport personality or of a respected member of the community. It is a name focused on the objective of the people it is intended to.

Name based on the decisions and choices people with special needs make in life.

Apart from their comparative disadvantages, they have the courage to fight to integrate to this world By stating: Here I AM, Heme Aqui, I am part of this world I want TO BE and I want to BELONG, that is why we chose this name.

There is a biblical passage when G'd calls Abraham and asks him: "Where are you? Abraham answers: HEME AQUI, HERE I AM.

So I wonder: how is it that if G'd sees and knows everything asks this question to Abraham?

By saying HEME AQUI, HERE I AM , Abraham is saying that he is present, not only in a physical way, but with his whole being, his consciousness, his spirit and his shape, just as the students of the school.

They are present not only in a physical way but they are also willing to fight for their rights, and giving the best of everyone, to stand up and state: HEME AQUI, HERE I AM.

Those who attend the school, to look for answers,

opportunities and challenges find in golf their way to transcend in society, to make it more fair and inclusive.

Thorns make roses bloom.

Each tournament they play, they discover themselves with love. ME and YOU transforming US.

INCLUSION AND INUSPSIQUIS

Inclusion of people with special needs, into the society and everyday life, shows us different ways of acceptance and how to name that acceptance.

Integration is typically mistaken by the fact of people with special needs and common people coexisting in the same common space, which is not right at all.

Considering the word integration, as a fundamental concept of mathematics, where an integral is the sum with an infinite number of addends, then in that case, we are using it correctly. People being in the same space, with a minimum contact but with not acceptance, is not integration.

In schools, if we say a person is integrated, just because he uses a small portion of a classroom but not considering the person as a whole, is not what we call integration.

Sometimes, a person with disabilities who works in an office, is not taken seriously by his work performance, but only based on affection.

In search of a word that would be more exact in its definition, the word Inclusion appears, which is the psychological acceptance of the other. Some doubts aroused about it, because it could refer to the mere intellectual acceptance without accomplishing the emotional acceptance.

Nowadays we can hear people talking about inclusion of minorities, but, is there a real acceptance? Who dares to challenge social pressure and say publicly how they really feel about it?

School of Life HEME AQUI, HERE I AM considers a person as a unity, in a social psychophysical spiritual way.

That is why words like Integration and Inclusion, are not

enough to describe our goal.

There is a need for a definition that would include the acceptance of the whole being. And is in golf, again, that we found the answer to this search.

People with special needs, play golf together with common people, in the same course, with the same elements, with the same rules in equal conditions.

By playing golf is that they learn about each other, they comprehend the other. Common people are able to experience along the game, the behaviour people with special needs have inside the course, their attitude in the golf course, and their achievements attained. From the intellectual point of view, common people are able to witness how much people with special needs, know about golf, and from the ludic point of view, a new relationship is established during the game.

Thinking about this idea of man as a unity, connecting with others as equals, is that we come up with the word INUSPSIQUIS*

People with special needs together with common people in the same room is not the real meaning of inclusion.

Psychologic acceptance is not enough, not by itself, not even the emotional part alone is enough.

In order for a real mind change to happen, there should be a real body, psyche, mind and spiritual- soul acceptance.

When does that happen? By playing golf in the same course, or by working together, on equal terms.

Acceptance goes through your skin into your guts, inside. (IN) Once inside, this acceptance goes to the "nous" soul-spirit (NUS) and finally to your PSYCHE.

The initial acknowledgment is done from the sense of reason, I accept the other, then I recognize him spiritually, from the unconscious and goes directly to the psyche-conscious side. In that exact moment is when you can say real inclusion happens, and the person is accepted as a whole human being and I called it "INUSPSIQUIS".[2]

Golf: its vision and its mission in Here I Am "Heme Aquí"

Vision: Training people with special needs as citizens and as golf players to play a leading role in changing society's mind. Achieving social inclusion for a more fair and equal society.

Mission: Use golf as a vehicle to achieve social inclusion between people with special needs and common people.

Golf empowers us to have a deep experience of love, evidenced in the progress of the possibilities and chances offered hidden behind restrictions. All the senses are important to connect with life and freedom. I decide about my life: showing my feelings of happiness and joy for the accomplishments attained in golf.

Heme Aquí Here I Am: Golf school Mentors

It is a great honour to have great masters of the Argentine golf as mentors.

Master Roberto De Vicenzo, winner of more than 200 international titles, renowned famous Man of Golf, not only for his sport spirit, but also his honourability and correctness in, and outside the course.

We were marvelled by his memory, regarding the school students, because he would always know how is everybody doing and everyone's achievement. He loved sharing long talks with the students and enjoyed their company. Roberto left us a lesson: You don't play golf as you wish you would, but as you can.

These kids play golf in their own way, but they sure play good golf, which will be of great help in their lives.

Golf will bring them joy and nice human relationships. Their improvement is remarkable. They can execute a swing by listening to songs and singing. Which I think is a very smart way of learning, resulting in great precise shots.

---

[2] *inside our spirit and our psyche.

* Term coined and registered by Nora Lelczuk

Vicente "chino" Fernandez is another mentor that contributes with the school and loves being with the students. He says: For me, golf, is like life: You learn every day.

And he quoted: never forget to enjoy life as much as golf, good shots, and good moments. And he adds; enjoy it, play it, have fun.

Eduardo "gato" Romero is an excellent golfer and another mentor of our school. Whenever he is playing in Argentina, we always go to watch him play. Whenever he realizes we are there, he steps out of the course, approaches one of the students and gives him or her a ball, knowing they would keep it with pride, and with their most important keepsakes.

First presentations of the school

In 1998 the School participated in a Congress about Isolation and Disabilities at The Universidad Católica de Roma "Catholic University of Rome"

In 2000, we made a trip with Vani to introduce the School at the Down syndrome Congress at The Down Syndrome Association in Washington causing surprised and admiration when she lectured. We also had the opportunity to talk about Heme Aqui School with the President at that time, Bill Clinton, at the White House.

In 2001, we lectured for the First Paediatrician Congress in Latin America. The same year the virtual Spanish magazine Down 21, wrote a note about our work. By December the same year Professor Jesus Florez published a long article about our school in the Scientific Magazine of Down Syndrome-

In 2002, we lectured on the 7th° Worldwide Congress about inclusion of children with disabilities.

In May 2003, we were invited to the talk: Mexico without barriers, and in December we were invited to the most important tournament of that country "Abierto Mejicano de Golf " Golf Mexican Open, to teach golf to Mexican young people with special needs and also to raise funds for altruist entities.

In 2004, the School was introduced at the Special Olympics, and at the Ministry of Special Education and other educational

Institutions in USA.

In 2007 a stand was held at the Ibero-American Congress for Down Syndrome with such a great impact, that led to open a School in Pinamar, in the Province of Buenos Aires.

Schools that use and practise "Heme Aqui "HERE I AM methodology in Argentina and abroad.

Apart from the main school, established at the Golf court of the Administration of the City of Buenos Aires, this methodology has spread, and is used in many other cities like: Mar del Plata, Tandil, Necochea, Bragado, Monte Hermoso, Berazategui, Campo público de Golf de la Armada at Villa Adelina (Buenos Aires) Public Golf court of the Army, Resistencia (Chaco) , Mendoza, Colonia, and Punta del Este, both in Uruguay. Santiago de Chile. Chile's Federation of golf also applies our methodology for teaching golf.

BASIS OF THE METHODOLOGY OF HEME AQUI

I found the meaning of life helping others find meaning in their lives.
Viktor Frankl

EDUCATIONAL GOALS
- Teach golf as a sport
- Inclusion trough integrated tournaments of people with special needs and common people.
- Tavision®: touch sense and vision sense to accelerate the comprehension and the learning of golf. *
- Activate®: recreation as a part of adjustment and coordination of the sport. *
- Nemomusic®: **Heme Aquí** Here I AM songs as a part of the main learning process. *
- Pargolf®: coordination exercises, concentration and posture. *
- Alogolf®: greeting as a way of social inclusion*[3]

SPORT GOALS
- Physical improvement, rotation improvement, mental alertness.
- Movement synchronicity.

SOCIAL GOALS
- Socialpeers®: establish a social connection. Group of belonging for students.*
- Socialparents®: establish a social connection. Group of belonging for parents.*
- Etigolf®: learning of ethics and moral principles.*

---

[3] * all Terms coined and registered by Nora Lelczuk. Original in Spanish also Activar® and Nemomúsica®.

- Playgolf®: dramaturgy to relate with other players in tournaments.*4
- Social support.
- Sport as a means of socialization.

STUDENT GOALS
- Desire of self-improvement.
- Strengthen self-esteem.
- Feeling of joy for finding a group of peers.
- Social success.
- Family recognition.
- Becoming protagonists.
- Play a very difficult sport.
- Development of new skills.

Staff required for the teaching of golf: Director, General coordinator, professor's coordinator, planning coordinator; sport Leader, golf professors, and junior sport leaders.

Heme Aqui has developed the most novelty and unique golf methods to teach their students.

Sport's Leader Junior Program: It's a two-year plan of studies, involving theory and practice with subjects that include: golf classes, its rules and etiquette, relationship between the sport leader and the students, communication abilities and their emotional connection with others.

When they finish the syllabus, they receive a qualification degree to be a Junior Sport Leader (LDJ), which enables them to work in HEME AQUI SCHOOLS.

Junior Sport's Leader work with 15 students, applying the Goldfinger methodology, they lead choreographies and exercises, while they keep learning. They are trained to teach to new students or to those that learn slowly.

---

4 * all Terms coined and registered by Nora Lelczuk. Original in Spanish also Sociopares®: and Sociopadres®.

It's a self-esteem encouragement work for them, because for the first time they are the teachers, not the students.

Goldfinger University Program

After two years of study, students received a qualification degree to be a trainer of the Goldfinger Method.

Our goal is to take golf to schools, institutions, universities, or business companies in order to become close and endear common people. In that way, people with special needs could demonstrate their achievements and abilities. Which is a great way to change minds and make society more fair and inclusive.

Latin American Summit Program

Once a year Heme Aqui Schools from abroad meet.

During that meeting, all students have the opportunity to meet with friends from schools of other branches.

Parents share experiences, families enjoy recreational activities like, a big dance, and of course, golf activities and playing golf out in the course.

At the end of the gathering, there is an unforgettable celebration, giving awards to all the young golfers that have attended the meeting, because they are all winners of life, thanks to HEME AQUI schools.

GOLDFINGER METHOD PEDAGOGY

We have developed a methodology of work by listening and analysing how people with special needs, connect and respond to the world. The Goldfinger Method is based on four grounds that mutually connect and strengthens each other.

Human Grounds
- Man as a bio-psyche-spiritual existence person, only comprehensible thorough transcendence.
- Help people to overcome their limits and appreciate

their present circumstances. Find a meaning.
- Discover their own freedom for personal benefits in their own life.

Social Grounds
- Recreational, social and cultural activities.
- Inclusion in social activities.
- Inclusion activities for parents and children.
- Talks to parents.
- Special guests.
- Trips.

Sports Grounds
- Teaching of specific physical education for golf.
- Inclusion exercises. Coordination and concentration.
- Included tournaments.
- Watch tournaments in which masters of golf are involved.
- Trips around the country to play included tournaments.

Educational Grounds
- Songs specially written to learn how to play golf.
- Team work to design the educational method.

School of Life Heme Aquí Here I Am: The School was founded as HEME AQUI, School of Golf for people with special needs, and later we developed a methodology of teaching, much more involved in their lives than a mere school of golf.

Golf is a means, a tool, to apply the Godlfinger methodology, which considers the human being as a unity.

HEME AQUI inclusion goal, considers physical, spiritual and psychological features of every human being, to teach this sport. This method could be used in every aspect of life. This method was developed taking into account all the concerns, wishes, and enquires of the students and their families, and from there on, we elaborated a methodology specifically design for people with special needs with a universal vision.

Why do we say it is universal? Because it was thought for the human being and its uniqueness.

Goldfinger method could be implemented before the specific teaching of any sport, as a method.

This methodology was created for the knowledge to prevail, and for the youngsters to be with their peers, to find their own abilities and achievements, and share experiences with others just like them.

This model is very demanding but committed, thought for the universality of the human being, considering all features.

Why teaching with this method? Because it causes changes for the good, that all students and families can validate.

Quoting Alfred Längle: it's a model that touches life itself.

TAVISION®

Teaching golf to people with minor or moderate mental disabilities has to attend every particular feature or difference existing among these people, in order for them to acquire concepts.

A golf course is immense and impossible to cover at a glimpse, so we proposed to walk it through in portions, using our sense of touch and our vision.

We use the sense of touch, for the student to feel and understand what lays ahead.

We walk around a hole showing every part and its names. The tee, the balls, the fairway or where the ball would go once the ball was hit, they touch the grass to see if it is high or low, and if it is soft, we locate the trees, the bushes, plants, the sky, the water, the sand, and we get to the green. We see its shape, we touch the grass again to see the differences, we recognize the flag, the hole, we measure it, to see if it is big or small, and we explain that the ball should go in there.

While we walk through, all the names learned are repeated,

playing with the speed of these repetitions, as a game to see who remembers them, or who says it first.

There are specific rules for every situation.

That is the purpose to know all the elements involved, in order to learn the rules later. We repeat this activity many times because of the difficulty and the quantity of the names, most of them in English.

It is advisable to make these activities outdoors but, If the climate were too cold or rainy, we would work indoors with magazines or stories, specially prepared, showing every part of the course.

In regards to the clubs, there are different "families": wooden golf clubs and iron golf clubs. Different clubs are used for different performances for different strokes and situations.

We make students touch the clubs to feel the differences, different shapes, textures and materials. We make students measure the clubs, and next we explain what every single club is made of and we learn about the club "families".

Later, on the golf course, we work with one club at a time to teach them how to use them, the range and speed needed for different clubs, and we teach them how to shoot too.

Another technique we implemented is, to use and incorporate their own bodies, not only to visualize, but also to feel what we are trying to teach them, like how to rotate the waist, and how to raise the club. We mark the position on the floor, we teach them how to relate things, and we teach them about tempo, which is the pace of a golfer's swing.

Mathematical concepts: golf has its own dynamics which allows us to learn mathematical and physics' concepts.

When I'm going to make a shot, I need to see where the ball is, if it is near or far from the hole, so I measure the distance. In order locate those measurements in space, and learn concepts I can relate along the game, like for example: The ball is closer to the lake but further from the hole, so I'm going to make a powerful but soft stroke.

I also work with additions and subtractions. For example, to make a specific shot, I chose the club that hits further but has a lower number. For example: if I'm 170 yards away from the hole, I have to hit further with wood drive 3, the further I have to hit the lower the number of the club. But if the ball is 80 yards away from the hole, the club I have to use is that of a bigger number like an iron 9.

Every time I'm going to hit the ball I have to pay attention to the orientation: to the right of the green, to the left of the hole, to the centre of the fairway. Everything depends on the point of view from where I am standing regarding the ball, which is related to the direction I want the ball to go, more to the left, less to the right etc. I also have to consider the speed, I want the ball to acquire, I have to pick a club according to the distance, and stand according to the direction I want the ball to head and calculate the strength and speed I want to impose to that shot.

Without even noticing I'm working with mathematical and physics concepts just before hitting the ball.

Golf, allows people with special needs, to assimilate concepts that are hard to learn in theory but through practice, they can analyse, visualize and incorporate them.

All these concepts are reinforced with concentration and coordination exercises.

There's a drill we practise by passing the ball, we say the right hand is the hand that we write with, and we pass the ball from the left to the right hand, and then we pass it to the friend on my right. Right foot in front, right hand up, and so on, with different instructions, to work with the sense of direction.

ACTIVAR®

Here we refer to the elements and recreational material we use in the school as a part of the learning process.

Educational material for the students.

We give the students instructional material for them to have their own golf paper material, with the golf rules adapted to their abilities, golf ethics, distance and range of the clubs used, golf elements, and golf course elements. We also work with figures and illustrations for them to learn concepts through questions and drawings.

At the beginning of the year, we hand out a calendar for them to mark, in it, school days, birthdays, tournaments, days they missed school, etc. The purpose is, not only to keep the student in touch with the group during the week, but also for visual stimulus, like color marks, so they can visualize their own participation, development in school and their achievements.

Parents also receive reading material concerning all kinds of different subjects, most of them about news that could contribute to the training, development, support and inclusion of the students. We work with parents and students to elaborate material related to the sport, like stories and games for them to reinforce what they have learned.

Training for Sport Leaders:

Educational material: golf has many elements to learn and remember. That is why we developed some material to make learning, easier. One of them is a golf story.

Here is how we use the teaching material: We put up a poster board with pictures simulating a golf course with water, bunker, clubhouse, trees, etc and we hand out to the students some elements, included in the story, previously cut and pasted to a paper. The sport leader begins to read, and as the story goes on, one of them approaches to the front, shows the picture to the students and pastes the element in its place.

Is important to read the story at a different pace every time, slower, faster, changing the order, adding new situations, to attract their attention and no to loose concentration.

Here is an example of the story:

A GOLF STORY

It was a beautiful February morning, and as the climate was so warm, dad suggested going to play golf.

As we arrived to the course, I started to recognize the place, and remember some things I have not seen, since I finished school. Look! There is the green! I can see the red flag from here! And over there, there is a man very focused on his game.

It looked like not everybody was on a golf break! And in some way I wasn't on a golf break either, because every time I played the golf songs at home, and started to dance in front of the mirror, in my head, I would picture Tiger Woods winking at me.

I was so distracted looking at the green, that for a moment, I left the golf club bag unattended and some clubs fell off, I picked them up, and dad didn't noticed it that all!

He looked very comfortable walking the course with those golf shoes he had for a long time. He liked to show them off, whenever he came over to see me playing in a tournament. Dad loved to come to the tournaments with me, not only because he was proud of me when I did a swing and hit the ball high, but also because he had the chance to meet "gato Romero" "Pato Cabrera" and "Roberto De Vicenzo ". Anyway, with or without his golf shoes, he was very happy to join me to the golf practise that day. After practising in the tee boxes and stretch a little, like Meli taught us, we went out to the course. Dad asked me, why don't we take those golf carts? and I said: the best part of golf is to walk the course and exercise, besides, I said, trying to convince him, we might run into Chino Fernandez today!!! I wouldn't like him to see me in the golf cart. He might think I'm lazy!!!

Dad understood that we were not in a tiring tournament, so we could enjoy the course by walking it through, and he did not ask any more questions.

At hole 3 I saw a boy from the other school, that was practising with the putter. At hole 5 I saw another of my friends with an iron club trying to get to the green, when I saw his ball and the club falling in the bunker, what a mess! And in another spot, were the people of HEME AQUI. Martín, Jaz, and Daniel that couldn't believe their eyes.

When we got to the hole 9. I was surprised to see Pato, standing right next to the bag of clubs, thinking how to get the ball in the hole with the putter, while Chino and Gato were walking the fairway having lots of fun.

I run into Santi, Eduardo, Maria Elis and Vani at hole 10 and said hello to them, they were paying attention to Roberto De Vicenzo that was explaining how to use an iron 8.

"Look! I think that Is Nora with a group of students getting ready for their physical training!"

"Oh my! Did they start without me?"

"I thought they did!"

We really had a good time, and by the end of the day, we were very tired! I was out of practice! And dad, haven't played for years! So we went to the clubhouse to have something to drink. I was so ready to finish my vacations and start my school year! I felt like getting together with my friends to tell them all the things I have done those months!

I also wanted to know what they have been doing, if they had time to play golf, if they had time to sunbathe, etc..

Suddenly dad asks me: "What are you thinking of?" And I thought, how do I answer to that? I was thinking about so many things! Clubs, flags, songs, bags, holes, green, laughter, swings, friends, exercises, bunker, but I just answered: "I think that I'm ready to start school this year!"

Dad smiled, and inside my mind, I kept singing the song: HEME AQUI, *here I am*....

I would love to have and ending for this story, but let me tell you that this, is just the beginning of the golf story we are going to share together this year at HEME AQUI.

Another educational material we work with, are golf magazines, to show the students the elements used in golf, like the clubs, for them to identify them, and learn what they are used for ,and how to handle them. We show students pictures of golf masters for them to recognize them, and inform them there are channels on tv about golf, and in that way they can get acquainted with golf players. We advise them to read the newspapers and search for pictures and news about golf tournaments to see the locations where they are being played. In this way, we can introduce the subject of the provinces they know, ask them if they've been in any of them, in order to see what they have learned so far.

Getting to know the golf clubs: The driver is the first club we use when we are at the tee, which is used for making long shots. The ball should be at the heel of my left foot. The woods

3, 4 and 5 are used to shoot from the fairway without tee, for long shots. Irons are used to propel the ball towards the hole, Irons typically have shorter shafts and smaller clubheads than woods, the head is made of solid iron. Iron 4, 5 and 6 are used to make long shots and sometimes are better than the woods.

The ball should be between my feet, at the centre. Iron 7 and 8 are used when we are near the green, 80 or 100 yards approximately, and are used for a precise shot.

Iron 9 is used when I'm 50 yards from the green and with a precise shot; I try to get to the green.

The pitch is used when we are very close or around the green. The ball should be at the right foot and I should make a backswing. If I use the pitch, it means I will have to have full control and be precise to take the ball to the green.

The sand wedge is used to hit from the bunker. I step firmly in the sand but be careful! I can't touch the sand with my club. I have to calculate how to hit the ball and then I make a backswing and I hit the ball in the sand.

The putter is used in the green. Head and feet still, I only move my arms like a pendulum, the club moves along from behind and forward on equal movements.

The woods: The drive is the longest club, then woods 3, 4, and 5. The lesser the number the longer the shaft, the bigger the number the smaller the clubface.

Irons: 4, 5 and 6 these shafts are shorter than the woods, but again rod 4 is shorter than 5 and so on.

The higher the number the more the clubface lays flat on the grass. / 7and 8 are shorter shafts, the clubface is wider more reclined, 9 has a short shaft and wide clubface, sand wedge: short shaft wide clubface and more reclined, pitch: very short shaft, clubface reclined, putter: is used in the green. In order to remember all the clubs I advise to make a parallel with the family. Woods: the drive is the father; wood 3 is the mother and 4 and 5 the sons. Iron 4 is the father 5 is the mother and the rest are the sons.

Training golf professors. Instructional material:

Instructions should be concrete. When we play in the green is very important to know in which direction to aim to get to the hole. To guide the students, we draw a big eva foam arrow, pointing the hole and lay it on the green, in that way it is easy for them to know which direction to hit.

Instructions for parents who join students in the golf course:

1. Every student should be at the tee with the tee, the ball and the club.
2. The ball should have a personal mark.
3. You should walk fast and play slow.
4. At the beginning, we tell them the number of holes, and where is the green, they are going to play at.
5. They should know how many strokes they made in every hole.
6. No more than two swing practise before hitting the ball
7. No talking or moving while a player is about to make a stroke.
8. No touching the sand in the bunker or they should suffer a penalty stroke
9. If the ball falls out of bounds it's a penalty stroke and it should be played another one from the same place as the one before.
10. If the ball falls in the water and is declared unplayable, a new one is played with a penalty from where the original ball was, before falling into the water.
11. You can look for a lost ball for 5 minutes, otherwise another one will be played with a penalty stroke.
12. If the ball falls on another players' line, it should be marked. After you finished the game, you should exit the course.
13. Sign the card at the end of the game.

NEMOMUSIC®[5]

Why do we use music to teach?

How does man communicate with the world? What are the elements man uses to communicate? Who understands him? Who comprehends him? How does he talk to himself? What are the means man uses to express himself? Is there a common language?

All of these questions arose, when we thought about how to communicate in an efficient way with people with special needs, and how to teach them all about golf and the complexity of this sport.

When we thought about how man communicates, we think of words and languages, but that, was not enough. We thought about painting as a means of expression, but we realized it was going to be difficult to coordinate so many colors. That's when we thought about music. My family and I always liked to dance, jazz, tap, tango cumbia, merengue, so we chose music as a means of communication. It just felt natural.

We also thought that if we could use our body to communicate, we should have excellent results in teaching golf.

For many centuries, music has been used by witches, kings, and Indian chiefs, as a means of expression to find the answers of the world's mysteries.

In king David's court, music, was known to have curative powers, and the Greeks thought, music, was relaxing and curative. In modern times man started to express his feelings through music.

Nowadays we use music together with our body, embodying heart and soul as a means of communication.

Music enables us to stimulate, educate and make changes, showing good results in people with special needs, however in order to pass on, all the ideas, and knowledge we had to use words in the songs.

We joined the voice with the body and the music altogether,

---

[5] And **NEMOMUSICA®** are **words coined and registered by Nora Lelczuk.**

and we found the perfect vehicle to pass on knowledge.

For these reasons is that the songs were specifically written with the purpose to teach golf to people with special needs.

People with Down Syndrome love to listen to music and dance and sing along.

They need to listen to it at high volume, like if they want to reach it and keep it inside themselves. They learn the lyrics very fast and they like to listen to them many times.

Students of HEME AQUI learn the songs and choreographies very fast, they like to show them when they get together at parties, and you can tell how much those songs mean for them and how they use them as a means of expression.

This is a very interested topic to develop, their ability to express.

Most of the people with Down Syndrome have difficulties in their speech, it's hard for them to pronounce, or sometimes they don't even speak at all. But there is no doubt that they can comprehend a great deal. This is the reason why music plays an important role. They can express themselves through their body movements, showing joy, enjoying the moment, reassuring their own world.

People without a specific diagnose have shown remarkable results with this method, helping them to coordinate and to improve their comprehension of instructions.

Leandro for example had difficulties with coordination, but as he learned the songs and choreographies, he managed to take control of his body and his coordination improved. His mother told us that he was very happy to attend our classes and liked it more than any other activity. His improvement was slow but steady and he got better at handling the clubs, he made progress on his posture and his swing.

Learning through music: Golf has many elements involved in the game. Unlike other sports, that you only need a ball to play, or a racquet, in golf you need gloves, balls, 14 clubs, a bag to carry them in, a towel, special shoes, tee, markers, etc

In other sports, the swimming pool, the football field, or the tennis court they all have the same shape and dimension every time, but in golf, every golf course is different, with different paths and different obstacles, making it hard to comprehend and remember.

Rules of this sport are numerous, complicated and hard to understand just like its etiquette rules.

We developed a methodology of teaching these rules through songs, written for this purpose.

We know teenagers are constantly listening to music, which makes it a very convenient means for them to learn.

- in a very fast and pleasant way.
- They can listen to the songs in any place and any time.
- Keeps them in touch with the school.
- Creates A feeling of belonging, since they identify themselves with the school anthem.
- Introduces golf etiquette in an easy way.
- They acquire basic rules of moral and ethical behaviour inside the golf course, through the songs.
- Songs are used as a means of presentation in social and cultural activities.
- Every song has its own specific choreography.

<u>Heme</u> <u>Aquí</u> <u>Here I Am song</u> : Takes the name after the school, and talks about how good it is to play golf together. Talks about how fun it is to learn to play golf, inviting to play this sport.

Music pretends to be like an anthem, very joyful and sticky. The lyrics talk about not being alone, being with peers and friends, having a group of belonging to share their accomplishments.

This song is the presentation of the school in any event and we also use it start the class.

<u>Gym</u> <u>for</u> <u>Golf song</u>: Physical preparation to play golf song: The aim is to train every part of their bodies to play golf. With this song, we exercise every part of the body, arms, waist, legs, and head.

The lyrics anticipate the part of the body we are going to work on. The song says, what are we going to move now? And the students answer. After all the exercises, the song ends up saying we are ready to play golf.

It's perfectly clear that this type of physical training, wants to instruct them always to exercise before the game. While they exercise, they follow instructions to reach a better concentration.

It is fun to play golf song: This song is used to teach all the different kinds of clubs and how to use them. The choreography of this rap is very demanding to what execution coordination and attention concerns. Students step to the front and they show the club, the way to handle it and how it is used. There is a silent space in the song, for them to say out loud what kind of stroke is made with each club.

The ludic side is always present when teaching this sport.

The swing's swing song:
We use the swing rhythm to teach how to swing and to make a good stroke.

We teach them how to stance, the position needed to handle the club, how to put their hands on the grip, how to position their legs and feet, how to make the downswing, how to hit the ball and move along with it, while their arms accompanies. And thus, getting closer to the green.

The Bad Guys (the obstacles) song: We call obstacles, the bad guys, because they were not invited, and we sing a song with spooky music about it. The song describes what a hole is, what a tee is, where and how I'm going to place the ball for the initial shot.

Then we introduce the fairway, a path with plants and trees on the sides. Later, bad guys are introduced. That is to say, the bunker, the water, and out of bounds. The song tells how to handle the situation if you end up in a bunker, tells about the penalty strokes .Then the green, where the hole is, and what to do. Mark the ball, clean it, look at the line, take off the flag, and of course make the ball to fall into the hole.

Golf is a sport with very strict rules and ethics, and in this song, we emphasize that.

There is no judge in this sport, so you have to be responsible for what you do; you have to count your own penalty strokes, and you have to stick to the rules, in order to beat the obstacles. This is a fun way for students to learn the rules.

They learn that the course has its difficulties, and as in life, you have to overcome obstacles.

The handicap song: This sport gives a comparative advantage to players according to their level. This song is for them to know the meaning of handicap. When we talk about handicap, we explain that golf offers an opportunity that not all other sports do. We also emphasize that the rival in this game is the course, not the players playing along with me as in other sports.

The rounded little one (golf ball) song:

It's a song to apply everything already learned in other songs. A playful music describes how beautiful the space around us is. Then we introduce the golf ball, small and round and how good we feel when we make a good swing, and we see the ball fly high (song N°4.) Then the song talks about the picking of the clubs to get to the green (song N°3) and tells you not to loose the ball like in song N° 5. This song also tells you to be careful with the ball because if it hits you it will hurt. With a cheerful music, we describe the beautiful space surrounding us in the golf course, the blue sky, and how good it feels when we see ball fly up high.

Relax: It's a song with a soft music saying that we are preparing our minds to play golf, we breathe, we focus, and we are ready to enjoy golf with joy in our hearts.

We recorded 2 CD's with the songs that are part of the study material of the school.

They are used to remember everything learned in class, and could be listened any time anywhere. It's a way for the student no to loose contact with the school and the teachers, havingt hose CD's at hand and by listening to them, they reinforce everything learned without having to wait a whole week for the next lesson.

We can prove by our experience that we attain excellent results by using music as a means of learning. Students are an active part of this learning process; they reaffirm their commitment to overcome the disabilities they were born with. As the song goes: "we will beat them!"

Heme Aquí Here I Am Anthem

Music and lyrics by Evelyn Goldfinger- Arrangements by Alberto Berbara. Educational content by Nora Lelczuk

Heme aquí, Here I Am
All together. Let's go now!
¡Come on! Let's go play golf.
What a lovely day for us to play together, Oh, oh, oh…
Go get your clubs and head for the field
Because it's golf what we feel!
We are gonna have fun
playing all together Oh, oh, oh…
Take your club with a lot of swing,
And say "hi" to the green!
Heme aquí, here I am
All together. Let's go now!
¡Come on! Let's go play golf.

PARGOLF®

Coordination and concentration exercises: The game could last between two to four hours, depending on how many holes the course has, demanding a lot of concentration time. Every hit demands focus and concentration, with many things to consider, the picking of the club, propelling the ball, the posture, making the swing right .All those things described before had to be taken into account without being distracted with what is going on around.

There is one very strict unwritten rule in this sport, and that is, whenever I see a player in position to hit, even though he might not be my game mate, I have to stop and make silence.

Golf Ethics considers respect for the others, a rule. Which is also valid for our everyday life.

What do I need to do in order to make a swing?

What does my body need?

What part of my body do I have to commit?

What abilities do I have to develop?

By playing golf, you will develop muscle tone. At the time of the strike, your body tightens shaping itself in a sport attitude.

Breathing plays an important role too; it needs to be relaxed and deep. The oxygen has to run through your whole body to make a good swing. You should remember that the swing is not about power; the more relaxed you are, the better the swing is going to be.

One of the weakest sides of amateurs is the lack of exercises before practising golf.

That is why in HEME AQUI we played the song "gym to golf" always before starting to play golf.

This practise produces vasodilatation, which increases the calibre of blood vessels, veins and capillaries. Making all the cardiovascular functions and the respiratory system to produce a bigger influx of blood to the muscles and better oxygenation of our body. Leaving us in a better condition, with greater energy to practise this sport, which is fully aerobic, preventing the muscles from suffering in a cold weather.

We need a fully developed body image to perform a swing, since we use the whole body, feet, legs, hips, waist, arms, hands, knees, neck, and head. Nevertheless some children of the school, did not had any body image at all, when they started, but through exercise, they began to developed a better body image. That was what happened to Edu.

It was very difficult for him to understand movement

instructions, it was hard for him to execute legs, arms and head exercises; he could not do the swing either, he could not handle the club correctly or any movement with it. Nevertheless thorough years of practice, he acquired a better posture, improved his body image and started to follow instructions of the exercises much better and in a precise way.

Another aspect of golf is the time-space location-awareness. Golf course is very large, so you have to locate yourself mentally and physically in that space. Then as we play, we need to know where to head to, locate the obstacles, the trees, and the boundaries. Every time you make a shot, you have to locate yourself in place and decide where to direct the ball. There are also great distances to cover and many obstacles to avoid.

First, you have to locate yourself in space, then, locate the ball and establish a triple relation between space-body, space-golf ball, and body-golf-ball. Once you are aware of your space location, then you have to consider where to direct the ball, knowing your arms are an extension of the club, to hit the ball correctly.

You have to relate all this things to internal and external time. Internal time is the one I need to get ready to hit the ball, and the external time, is given by other players.

I should not delay my game, because that implies delaying others` game. This temporal relation combines with golf ethics, because whenever I'm delayed in the game, I have to give way to other players behind me.

Our notion of direction is always present in golf, when I'm standing facing the ball, pointing either to the left, right or center, during the swing, I turn my shoulders, hips and arms to the right, and later hit the ball and turn to the left.

It is interesting to see their fine and gross motor coordination improvements. They progressed on the way to handle the clubs, and their hands and finger position. As to gross motor coordination concerns, we had great results on their rotation exercises, which include hips, head, shoulders wrists and hand movements. We know that this kind of exercises are mostly applied on every physical therapy treatment.

Our method demands focus and concentration and we

practice very hard to make it work. Our methodology implies clear instructions about the need to concentrate. We can walk and talk through the course during the game, but at the time of hitting a ball, we should be focused.

Once I had the chance to see Gato Romero and Pato Cabrera encouraging and congratulating themselves over a good putter.

Why do we practise the swing once, before hitting?

Because there are so many different clubs to choose from, and because every single one is for a different purpose, that you have to concentrate after every strike, to pick the right club, for every situation.

Coordination is very important for the swing. Swing is about tempo, and making the right movements, is not about strength, force or power.

Power is the consequence of performing a good swing, coordination of arms, legs, hips, and head, leads to the perfect moment to hit the ball. Having in mind not to get distracted by people's voices or movements going around.

You have to talk gently and softly to people with special needs for them to comprehend. Explaining that the whole movement has to be synchronised, and in that way, they understand that the best shot is the one made with swing.

In order to achieve a better coordination, we exercise the parts of our body, needed to play golf. Exercises of flexibility, rotation, breathing, coordination, concentration, body image, time-space location, side movements, fine and gross motor skills just to make a good shot, and not to mention climate conditions, mood of the students, etc.

There is no time to think about the last shot I made, if it was a good one or a bad one, I have to focus on the next one, and keep on going, just like life itself.

These exercises of concentration, coordination, integration, rotation, mental skills, socialization, group behaviour, and respect for the rules, are tools that help to prepare students for inclusion, working inclusion or as complement at work. It also contributes to encourage their learning process and reinforces social behaviour.

HEME AQUI students have the opportunity to watch great masters of golf playing tournaments, which works as a natural stimulus, wanting to emulate them in some way.

ALOGOLF®

Welcoming: The initial salute is a part of the methodology used at HEME AQUI SCHOOL. Is one of the rules of golf.

When I'm out in the course, I greet my friends and say my name together with my handicap.

By greeting others, we show respect for others, we show that we care, that we consider others, giving us the chance to start a fluent dialogue.

Why do we think greeting is important?

Very often, we enter a place and salute only the people we know; saying hello to everybody is something not very usual.

As when we take a bus and say hello to the driver, do we all do that?

If you do, you will notice the driver will be surprised and he will have a different attitude. Driver will feel recognized feeling not only like a mere anonymous person driving a bus.

Why do we need to be greeted? What is the intention?

By greeting we show education, and respect, significance and consideration for the other person.

Salutation happens on every sphere. By greeting we show an intention, a movement, either by gestures or spoken.

I express myself, I move with an intention to talk to others looking for a response, that could be answered or not, but every time looking for a response to my greeting which might cause and action and a reaction.

Depending on the way I salute, I move my hands, my arms, my head, my mouth, my cheeks, my eyes. I move parts of my body structure.

Heme Aquí greeting: -By greeting we introduce the school to the students, we show them that they belong to the school and they are part.

-This is a way to tell them that the activities begin.
- Is the moment they meet again with friends and professors.
-- Is the moment when they share all the news they might have.
-Everyone has their moment to express themselves.
-They love to hear about friends that went to a tournament and they comment about it. The get motivated about it.
-Bonds are reassured
-They realize if someone is missing class.
-They have a sense of community in HEME AQUI.

Our body is considered the most wonderful example of G'ds creation. We have one body, and we have to take good care of it, because we communicate with it and through it.

We have to feed our body in order to fill the spirit, and not to be a burden. A body which sometimes makes us proud, and which sometimes makes us worry.

Body worship is a problem in our postmodern society. In this monotheist society, sometimes other gods appear that want to run our lives, like GOD Hedonism, the pursuit of sensual pleasure; materialistic God, the cult of money; body worship, sculpted beautiful bodies, with no spirit, no sense; isolated bodies in multutide and celebrated… in isolation.

When students arrive at the school, they are greeted with a hug and a kiss by their professors; communicating through body gestures and movements, that they are all important.

They are persons that go to school because they want to succeed in their lives, to be with friends and to share together the experience of this motivational activity.

We like to pay attention to any physical change in the students, like a new haircut, or if he or she looks nice, in order to be supportive, and say it out loud. And we pay attention to adults too.

The goal is to make them feel they are considered, and is important and is taken into account, if someone is present that day or not.

That is how relationships grow and become strong among them, teaching with affection and care, generating open doors to the unknown, where stories are developed, and attitudes appear beyond expectations.

<u>The hug:</u> When we hug and kiss, we initiate a salute much more committed, joining intention, gestures, movements, that involves my body, and myself. I react in an experienced way, I establishing a connection with the other, which means being with the other.

When I greet with only a word or with a gesture I'm rationalizing it, I don't establish a connection.

When we hug, we touch, and by touching the other one's body, is like being the other. Touch the other one's heart, that are touched with our actions, reaching souls.

Nowadays we live in an individualist society, where everyone is alone. We are used to connect with others through the intellect, but we are still empty in a world of no affections.

But whenever we hug and touch, a new dimension opens.

I'm committing myself to connect with others.

Many activities, workshops and schools nowadays are giving the importance of touching its real place, as a way to be acquainted with others.

Alfred Langle, President of the Logotherapy Society in Viena, wonders: What happens when we touch? Our life is touched. What happens when we get close? Our heart is touched.

Something inside changes, the core of all our affections and feelings is the source where the feelings grow.

We can conclude that a feeling is the fact of being touched, and that, is life itself.

At Heme Aqui, hugging is touching, is telling the students that we are together, here, with our bodies. Is telling them here lies the affection and care with which I'm going to teach you today. That is how confidence is transmitted. This hug is full of energy and affection for you. And they respond with joy because they are aware that they are important and feel that affection.

And if there is one student that does not want to hug or kiss, doesn't matter, we have to try anyway and wait with patience.

This is the case of Claudio. He didn't want to kiss, or hug or talk with women. But as time went by, and as he made progress in golf, he began to feel part of the school. Claudio took his time and slowly began to accept being hugged or kissed, and today he greets and talks to his professor. And if he makes a good shot, he jumps of joy and hugs me.

Every time María Elis arrives, she likes to play the game of covering my eyes and ask, guess who?

Melisa likes to hide behind a tree to call the attention, and later she runs to hug me.

Students also hug each other, even though some could be a little shy and just say hi, they all greet each other with no exception. In order to reinforce this greeting idea, we all sit down in a circle, where they all say hi and everybody answers.

SOCIALPEERS®

Students' Group of belonging: At the HEME AQUI School we work on a social-cultural sport basis.

By Performing this Social activities we seek to reassure their group of belonging through inclusion activities.

We celebrate birthdays, National holidays, mother's day, family day, spring day, Christmas etc. Meetings take place at the golf's clubhouse, with music, food cooked by parents, and handmade presents, for the students. We also celebrate every birthday of the students. Last November, there were four different birthdays to be held, and Lucho suggested celebrating the four of them together at a bowling alley, they all agreed, and had lots of fun playing bowling, eating and dancing. Parents were happy too.

Students also meet outside the golf school sphere. They like to go dancing or to the movies as extra activities. They enjoy going to museums, or theaters, as a cultural activity, inviting common people to join them.

As a social inclusion exercise, they all sit together in a circle, where they would comment about all the subjects they are interested in, news they want to share about school, work, other sport they practise, other activities they are involved in, or if someone participated in a tournament or if they made a trip.

Regarding the specific sport area activities, they attend tournaments to watch professionals play; and they participate on integrated tournaments in different golf courses and also travel to other provinces for the same purpose. These trips give them the possibility to meet new friends and reassure their sense of belonging.

SOCIALPARENTS®

Group of belonging for parents: Parents are an important part of the methodology at HEME AQUI. They find the school as a group of belonging too. A place to share their concerns and talk frankly without being judged. The place where they meet, the golf club, is a beautiful location surrounded by an open green space and fresh air. They feel happy about having found a place of their own, a place to share their experiences and stories. .They are parents with the same concerns, questions and problems about the future of their children, and they share and comment experiences and information that might be useful to each other. Parents are going through the same process of walking the path of learning about disabilities, transforming the relationship among them for the better, because they understand and comprehend each other.

They go to the golf club to find their friends and they have their own meetings, birthdays and BBQ together too. They take their children to play golf but they have a good time too.

Students themselves were the ones that showed their parents a new social life, giving their families the opportunity to be open to something new. They relate to other parents out of positive feelings, sharing their children achievements, and celebrating it together.

Surrounded by these people, in this environment, is that you achieve significance. Where the other, is part of my story and part of my life, sharing ideas and feelings.

ETIGOLF®

Sports and Ethics:
What do you think of, when you think of sports?
Sports are activities that include physical, psyche, social, ludic, competitive, aspects, each one having its own pace, played in groups or individually, amateur or professional. Sports demand training, dedication, care, willingness, commitment, honorability, loyalty, honesty and team spirit. All sport's principles. What kind of principles?
Principles to perform a sport in a right, honest and fair way as possible.
These are some guidelines and principles on which good athletes are based on.
 Behave correctly during the game,
 Being a good loser,
 Be a good teammate, and help others.
Recognizing one's faults or flaws, is called honesty. Training and exercising often is called sacrifice.
We choose our principles and we behave accordingly, we apply them in our everyday activities and we choose to live by them, to give life a meaning.
Viktor Frankl calls it "attitude principles "
What attitude do we assume when facing what life has put us through?
Do we get depress because we fail to achieve our goals, or do we make an effort to accomplish it?
Do we have an incorrect behaviour if we fail, or do we face it with dignity?
Every attitude towards a game or our life tells and shows the principles we live by.
Principles are present in every sport, but in golf these principles are written, and are as important, as rules themselves.

Ethical Behavior: Golf has, among its principles, an ethical behaviour rule, which suggests how you should behave once you enter the golf club, until you leave it. Behaviour inside the golf course should be impeccable.

These written rules are called golf Etiquette .If a golfer does not comply with the rules, he will not have a penalty in the game, but he will have a moral sanction penalized by other golfers.

Even though the course has a great extension, and you might be alone, during the game you should always behave correctly, even if no one is watching. This is the reason we emphasise, that the students should know golf Etiquette, and play by it, because this habits are also suitable for life.

During the game, there are moments to talk and moments to keep quiet. Whenever a player is about to make a shot, we should keep quiet and still, no to disturb his game. Never forgetting he needs a lot of concentration to hit the ball, because a bad stroke is one more point to write down on the card. We teach them, that team spirit and behaviour in this case, is very appreciated and valued.

There would be situations where we might loose a ball or just walk slow, causing to delay the game. In that case, we should leave way to other players behind us, not to delay their game too, and although this is not compulsory, this is what a good player does. This is called value of courtesy.

In golf, every player is responsible to take down notes on the game's card. He should write how many shots he made to take the ball to the hole. Is up to the player to write the correct score.

During tournaments there are scoreboards but we have to keep the score anyway.

That principle is called HONESTY.

Students always want to win, that is why we should keep them in mind, how important it is to enjoy the game and compete.

There is a story about going to see the masters of golf play a tournament at the Jockey Club Argentino, and we all approach to say hello to master Vicente Chino Fernandez.

Vanina approaches him and says:

"Did you know Chino, that the most important thing of a sport is to compete? Right?""

Fernandez looked at her and said: "Well, yes of course!!!"

After a short silence, Vanina insists: "But winning is better, right?"

Chino laughed out loud!

It is very important to work with those feelings, because students tend to feel bad after a tournament, if they don't win. They are in a bad mood or they start to cry, when they should be enjoying. This is what we call players' behaviour principle.

It is important to emphasize to the students, that without any effort there are no achievements or rewards, emphasizing the importance of practice, to obtain good results.

We advise them to watch the masters of the golf and professionals play, for them to know all the dedication they put into this sport.

This is what we call effort and perseverance Principle.

Leaving the course in the same conditions as it was before playing, and cleaning after, is called Respect for others and the environment Principle.

At HEME AQUI we teach and underline all those Principles, and In order to pass them on to the students we do it in a theatrical way.

We act situations and then, they talk about how they felt about it, if they got upset about something, or how they dealt with a situation. The goal of these dramatizations is to incorporate habits and principles of this sport, in a clear and dynamic way. Later to be applied on the game or in life itself.

PLAYGOLF®

Training for social and sport encounters: When someone meets a person with special needs, it is difficult to start a connection or a conversation for the first time. People often don't know whether to talk to them or not, or how or what to say.

At HEME AQUI, we organize golf tournaments with inclusion in which there will be interactions between people with special needs and so call common people. Conversations such as what club to utilize or the direction in which to hit the ball may arise. Or any other type of dialogues. At Heme Aqui we give the students the necessary tools to be prepared to talk and even to act first, whenever these situations arise.

HEME AQUÍ HERE I AM FOUNDATIONS

He who has a why to live, can bear any how.
Friedrich Niezstche

Our educational methodology is based on the anthropological, existential, psychological and educational basis of Viktor Frankl, who developed the concept of Logotherapy.

Logotherapy is founded upon the belief that striving to find meaning in life is the primary, most powerful motivating and driving force in humans.

These foundations define man related to intention in search of values as a motivation that would stimulate psycho-affective impulse through golf.

These motivations express, in the words of Dr. Frankl:

Yes to life in spite of everything.

EDUCATIONAL LEVEL

Educational stimulus to learn is made through music, songs, coordination exercises, and motor and location concentration, with a ludic attitude. In an environment of joy, team spirit and stress free, surrounded by green open areas.

The students learn and feel happy, and they like the songs so much, that they take them home with them as a CD, to sing them over and over to keep learning.

Sometimes at a birthday party, they like to play the songs and dance along as a game.

They assure that the exercises are dynamic, and stimulating. Sometimes when we introduce, new exercises they have no problem to incorporate them, besides the difficulties they might present.

There are new subjects of interests that call the student's attention, like watching golf on tv, learn about new players, read golf magazines and most of all, be a principal actor when they are interviewed on tv, together with their admired golf master.

Activities are approached with joy and fun, but also with effort, discipline and respect for the assignments. Leaders are accepted, valued, loved and respected, they are known as " the people that help them grow".

Once the learning process is incorporated, it becomes an art, leading to knowledge beyond golf, where the efforts made, become real, and that is the moment when they stand up and express: HEME AQUI, HERE I AM.

The group responds with a high level of positive results to what experiences, creativity and attitude concerns. Students improve their fine and gross motor skills and location skills, their concentration and coordination; acknowledged by the way they handle the clubs, their movements, their turns and rotation, their feet coordination, legs position, waist movements, shoulders, arms, hands and head coordination and their walking. Through trial and error students worked in a specific concrete way, as when they perform their golf exercises.

They learned that through comprehension and reasoning they are able to assimilate the habits that this sport requires.

They are happy, for the achievements attained, and for their new relationship with their peers, a bond strong enough that allows them to overcome obstacles together.

We can observe from the attitudinal point of view, a behavioural change towards their feeling of freedom and willingness. Inside the family environment, they show a much more positive and spontaneous relationship, reaffirming family's rules. Parents are amazed at their children improvements, generating a feedback of feelings. Parents begin to see their children from a different perspective, and experiencing their love in a different way. Reflecting themselves on the achievements accomplished. Expressing, "life is wonderful!"

CREATIVE LEVEL

Whenever an obstacle appears, people with special needs, develop a strategy, which goes beyond the specific given instruction, appealing to their creativity to try to learn it; they play, as a way of learning.

Creativity joins with effort, intuition and precision. Using their creativity to accomplish the goal besides the technique, trying trial and error to transcend together with the sport and its real meaning.

The students begin to have a sense of freedom, they feel creative and knowing they can achieve golf objectives.

ATTITUDINAL LEVEL

When we talk about attitudes, we talk about how we face life.

We can observe positive attitudes in students; they show their happiness before others, and their feeling of joy for having established strong bonds with their peers. They have a group of belonging, they identify themselves when they wear their school uniform, and they are seen, not as people with different needs, but as golfers, playing tournaments with common people, showing their readjustment, their self-improvement and their attitude towards life.

Attitude change is accomplished by social interaction through communication. Viktor Frankl calls it "a common point", when two or more people go beyond their love, they both have the same reason to live, with the purpose of making something real every day.

This is the meaning we confer to play golf.

TESTIMONIES

For only to the extent to which man commits himself
to the fulfillment of his life's meaning,
to this extent he also actualizes himself.
Viktor Frankl

Nora,
I'm about to be eighty-three years old and I have read many books about golf in my life. Nevertheless, I have not been able to figure out all the secrets of golf, but you are so special, that I'm sure you will. Roberto De Vicenzo

HEME AQUÍ
Tango
Mrs Goldfinger,
I want to thank you for this school,
which has the intention to bring joy to the children,
with this sport.
Your effort is going in the right direction.
Children are coming to the performance,
together with Master Roberto and Chino Fernandez
whom give their support with all their love.
Playing the game, children enjoy
Allowing them to think and act
It is very necessary to play, and for many reasons
This sport is intended to find friends
That is why this school gathers friend together, to play.

I dedicate these lyrics to Mrs. Nora Lelczuk, the founder of this Golf School for people with special needs, joined together by this wonderful sport that is golf, with all my affection, to Mrs. Nora Goldfinger.
                    Manuel Nicolás Sierra de los Padres Golf Club

Testimonies from parents

It's possible to affirm that parents have gone through three different stages.

1- Amazement and surprise for the practise of this sport, appreciation of the methodology and the analysis of the results obtained by their children.

2- Appreciation for the Inclusion achieved through integrated tournaments of golf.

3- the group of belonging their children accomplished in this school and the importance that golf gained in their lives; since most of the student's social life is based on the activities, the school offers.

Parents have gone under a similar experience as their children, because they consolidated a group of belonging too.

It has been two years since Leandro is coming to the school, and it has been a before and after school experience, a milestone in our lives. By saying our lives, I mean the whole family group.

Leandro has improved his posture not only during the game but also in his everyday life.

He improved his sense of space-location (left, right, ahead) and his coordination of movements. Leandro is now able to focus on the direction of the hole and hitting the ball at the same time.

Additionally he has applied everything he has learned in school in other areas of his everyday life too.

His behavior has improved, now he takes his time to follow instructions given by his professors, and accepts all remarks made to him. He is a very anxious and active boy and he gets distracted easily. His periods of attention are short, but he has improved, he can concentrate longer and his performances are better, which leads him to improve his self-esteem, which encourages him for achieving his goals, making him happy. It is all a chain of successions, which are beneficial for Leandro, either in a practical or emotional way.

Golf School Heme Aqui not only has taught Leandro how to play golf, but represents an environment where to develop himself as a person.

Director's concern to play inclusive games with common people, makes a valuable experience, for everybody. She puts every effort to demonstrate others the possibility people with special need have to overcome difficulties and to put aside all differences that might separate them.

Finding a supportive group where to belong to, is one of the most important achievement of the school, where parents grow and learn from new experiences. Allowing inclusion for the rest of the family in order to share activities with Leo. Brothers, sisters, grandparents they all have the possibility to open their hearts and be aware of the situations Leandro faces, and in that way they can support him and see everything from another perspective. Leandro's self-esteem has gone greater than ever because now, he has the chance to show his accomplishments and then, apply them in other areas.

The School HEME AQUI HAS BEEN THE PLACE where Leandro found a place to be, to grow with respect, love and equality.

Lic. Laura Cardona de Petrauskas

Mrs. Lic. Nora de Goldfinger – Mr. Luis Goldfinger

The undersigned by mutual agreement send this written acknowledgment to Mrs Nora Lelczuk Goldfinger and Mr Luis Goldfinger to express our most deeply appreciation for the work done with our children.

The above mentioned Nora Lelczuk and Mr Luis Goldfinger, Directors of HEME AQUI SCHOOL for people with special needs, are carrying out an innovative work, to what social inclusion of our children concerns. They are the authors of a Golf School for people with special needs one of its kind. Supported by the Administration of the City of Buenos Aires and the Golf Club, our children learn golf with amazing results. Based on these achievements attained, is that we want to express how marvelled we are. We want to express as parents and students our gratitude to you both and warm wishes.

Alfredo González y Familia

I want to say, that, besides been the 10th time I listened to that CD, I have to confess that the first time I listened to it, I thought Luciano would never be able to follow the instructions in it.

But when he listens to the CD he loves to ask me to watch him perform those golf movements; he stands in a straight position to hit the ball, his hands behind his head and turns the waist to both sides.

Then he smiles and asks me: are you listening too?

He was listening to the song " small" . The song talks about a club for short shots, but when I ask him if he knew the names of the clubs, he gets angry, takes off the CD and says: No, I don't know.

I thought that if Lucho didn't know the names of the clubs, it could be a problem for him at the school.

I talked to Nora about this, because she always listens and I tell her that he is not a conventional boy, that his pathology is aphasic .He understands, and the answers are in his head, but he just cannot verbalize them. He has good motor skills; he loves sports, cycling, swimming, horseback riding and golf. He is very sociable and found in golf a group of belonging since all the other sports he practises are individual sports. Luciano is very happy to attend classes and go out with the youngsters to Mc Donald's to share his lunch. He is very affective with his friends and parents. I wish he would always be a part of this school, it means a piece of happiness for him.

Hebe Gonda

Golf improved Charly's life. We are aware that his concentration improved, he takes his time to execute instructions, and he can deal with anxiety and follow the rules. Motivation is an important feature for Charly. Golf with his peers is very motivating. We are proud to be part of HEME AQUI. Thank you, Nora!

Silvia Guglielmino

Testimonies of people that played integrated tournaments.

This is the method we use for integrated tournaments: first drive made by a student of the school and then a common player follows. We choose the best ball. First hit is important. One father of joins the students in the course to keep the scores.

Performance of the students was a surprise for the other youngsters, who celebrated their peers' accomplishments.

At the end of the game, Director of HEME AQUI, made a survey to be answered freely, by common people who played golf along the students to evaluate, to what extent, playing golf with people with special needs, generates changes.

1. Have you ever played with people of HEME AQUI School before?
2. What do you think now?
3. Would you like to play with them again?

Here are the exact answers:

They are very good at it and more affectionate than we are. They are not disable at all. When I first saw them I thought they were not physically able to play golf, but now I think they are!!

Federico

They have the same learning skills as we have, and they have a really good behaviour inside the course.

Nacho

I have played with them before. They are nice, and they show their affection to others. Their coordination improvements are excellent. I was told I could play with them last year, it's fun.

>Matías

I like that they integrate with us, they can, and they must keep on.
>Juan Manuel

I didn't know them before. They are smart. They have good memory. It's fun.
>Sebastián

They are like everybody else. Nice and warm.
>María Pía

It's a good thing how a boy, different from me, learns to play golf.
>Francisco

It's a good thing that people with special needs are able to play golf and I like to watch them play.
>Matías

It's fun to watch them play, I didn't know they could play this good. They show they are able to blossom in many areas.
>Juan

They should keep playing this good.
>Germán

They are enthusiastic with the game, they don't care about the score, they play for fun, they are very clever.
>Francisco

They play really well. Their future is promising.
>Matías

Hernán and Florencia Gelay are parents who joined them at the game and said:

They are so stimulated, and they are smart. I was surprised that they remembered all the names. They are not disabled. They have another kind of intelligence. They are very affectionate. They have no evil intention at all.

Answers show, that golf, acts like a "mind changer", contributing for an opportunity to get to know each other.

As we said before; you begin playing with a disabled person and end up playing with a person. This is what we observe in tournaments. Common people enrol to play with people with special needs, just for the fun of playing golf for a while, not knowing what they will find. Along the game, common people begin to realize all the skills people with special needs have, and their learning ability, their respect, and their joy, waking up to realize that they feel and live too, just like anybody else.

That is the moment when amazement arises, when being faced to an unknown situation, which is to learn and to share with others a different reality. An experience that motivates and causes personal growth, changes of thoughts, changes of rules, and attitudes, resulting in a very deep experience. Which later will develop in greater consequences along their life, in order to achieve a more fair society.

It is clear evidence that the Goldfinger method used by HEME AQUI school is to develop abilities of people with special needs, create a framework to have a group of belonging as citizens and sportsmen, through golf, in order to accomplish social inclusion for a more fair and supportive society.

HEME AQUI players, act responsible to make this goal a reality.

They make an effort to learn this sport, a very demanding and difficult one, with joy and to be able to share his accomplishments with others, and with the purpose to give their lives a meaning.

Max Scheller calls this "situation principles"; principles showed in a given situation, at a certain given moment in history, at a certain time. A situation with a real person showing his attitude towards others and transcend, to give life a meaning.

NORA LELCZUK CV

EDUCATION

Degree in sociology, University of Buenos Aires 1970.

Piano Professor, music theory, 1968.

Educational Logotherapy and existential analysis, 2005.

Life coach, Coaching Degree and Ontological Process Degree, acknowledged by International Coach Federation, 2019.

TEACHING

University of Buenos Aires, philosophy school. Sociology.

Teaching assistant in statistics, 1970-1971.

Teaching assistant at Economic Science University, introduction to sociology, 1971.

Statistics Department UBA, 1984-1992.

Founder of HEME AQUI for people with special needs, education and integration through golf, 1999.

Director at HEME AQUI Argentina, Uruguay, and Israel.

Founder of the Goldfinger method, 2000.

Director and founder of the Goldfinger University for people with special needs, 2014.

Founder and coordinator of reflexive women's space, 2001.

MEDIA WORK

Producer at a radio program for teenagers at Be Iajad, Radio Jai, 1994.

Host of short program called " nuestro tiempo", from woman to woman, cable tv, 1994.

Interviewer of a cable tv program," tiempo de paz ", 1995-1997.

Producer and host of the radio program " Nuestro interés", radio Shalom, 1995.

WORK IN INCLUSION OF PEOPLE WITH SPECIAL NEEDS

Co-author of the integration project a way of life, to include people with minor disabilities to Jewish schools, 1995.

Participant of the Committee to integrate people with special needs, to common schools, 1995-1997.

Author of the first School of Golf for People with Special Needs, 1999.

Founder of the program Junior Sport Leader, 2012.

Founder of the Goldfinger University for People with Special Needs, 2014.

Founder of the workshop for People with Special Needs, thoughts from freedom, 2017.

PUBLICATIONS

Golfsinger by Goldfinger

Educational songs recorded on CD for HEME AQUI SCHOOL.

LECTURES ABOUT THE GOLDFINGER METHOD

VI Congreso Internationale: Isolamiento e Handicap. Universita Catolica del Sacro Cuore. Roma. (1998)

National Sindrome Down Association. Washington. EEUU. (2000).

Primer Congreso Argentino de Discapacidad en Pediatría y Primer Congreso Latinoamericano de Discapacidad en Pediatría. "El Golf como Vehículo Integrador". Buenos Aires, Argentina. (2001).

"Heme Aquí, el deporte como factor de inclusión". México sin Barreras. México, DF. (2003).

"El golf y la inclusión" Board of Cesarea Golf. Israel. (2010).

"Metodología Goldfinger" Club Curitibano de Golf, Asociación Síndrome de Down de Curitiba y Universidad de Curitiba. Brasil. (2008).

"Los valores, la ética y la conducta humana en el golf y en la vida". España. (2010).

"El método Goldfinger, herramienta para el grupo de pertenencia". Federación de Golf. Chile. (2010).

"El ser humano mirado como una unidad" Institución La

Huerta. Campo de Golf Sheraton Colonia. Uruguay. (2010).

"Heme Aquí y el golf como herramienta" Federación Uruguaya de Golf. Uruguay. (2010).

"Heme Aquí, historia de vida" Asociación Síndrome de Down y Municipalidad de Maldonado. Uruguay. (2010).

"El método Goldfinger como herramienta para el desarrollo de la persona humana" Club del Lago. Uruguay. (2010).

"El deporte como vehículo de integración". Universidad Católica Argentina. Fundación Río Colorado. Argentina. (2011).

"El sentido como herramienta" IV Congreso de Logoterapia. Argentina. (2011).

"Método Goldfinger, su alcance en la vida de los jóvenes con discapacidad intelectual". Academia de Golf Jean Mc Lean. Miami, EEUU. (2011).

"Pedagogía Heme Aquí, la relevancia del grupo de pertenencia". Rotary Club Recoleta. Buenos Aires. (2011).

"Heme Aquí, escuela de vida" Academia de Golf Jean Mac Lean. Miami, EEUU. (2012).

"El Método Goldfinger, su pedagogía y su aplicación teórico-práctica". Para los Profesionales de Golf de Argentina. Buenos Aires, Argentina. (2012- 2015).

"Golfterapia y la persona humana". Congreso de la World Mental Federation. Buenos Aires, Argentina. (2014).

"La Biblia y la Discapacidad" , Limmud, Miami, EEUU.(2015)

"Heme Aquí, el golf y su implicancia práctica". Charlie De Lucca Development Center. Miami, EEUU. (2014- 2015).

"Discapacitados o Personas" Congreso de Logoterapia Buenos Aires, Argentina. (2015).

"Los Jóvenes Fragmentados" Congreso de Salud Mental. Buenos Aires, Argentina. (2015).

"Lo No-Verbal y el Golf", Congreso de Comunicación No-Verbal. Porto, Portugal (2019).

"La verdad y la mentira es una misma cosa", Congreso de Logoterapia El Hombre como Punto de Encuentro, Buenos Aires, Argentina (2019).

COACHING AND TRAINING

HEME AQUI Methodology, Sports and Disabilities, AMIA, Argentina, 2006.

Disability and Inclusion, Golf Club Acantilados, Mar del Plata, Argentina, 2007.

HEME AQUI school of Life, training for golf professionals, schools' Directors and parents, Resistencia, Chaco, 2007.

Sport as a tool for inclusion, San Luis Government, San Luis, 2007.

Goldfinger method in HEME AQUI, Golf Club Colón, Colón, Entre Ríos, 2007.

The Social group as the main structure for human progress, Pinamar Golf Club, Argentina, 2007.

Coordination and concentration exercises, Necochea Golf Club, Necochea, Argentina, 2008.

Sport as a tool for inclusion, Monte Hermoso, Argentina, 2008.

Principles, ethics and human behaviour in golf and as in life, Berazategui Rotary Club, Buenos Aires, Argentina, 2008.

Goldfinger method deeply analysed, Golf Club Carmelo, Uruguay, 2008.

Music as a means for studying, Golf Club Bragado, Buenos Aires, Argentina, 2009.

ACTIVAR, activities to socialize in sports, Colonia, Uruguay, 2009.

Sport as a tool for inclusion, Golf Club Valle Escondido, Tandil, Argentina, 2009.

Rotation, concentration and coordination exercises, Sheraton Golf Club, Colonia, Uruguay, 2010.

Goldfinger educational strategy: etiquette and principles, behaviour in sports, Buenos Aires, Argentina, 2010.

HEME AQUI sports and challenges, Santiago de Chile, Chile, 2010.

Goldfinger method, educational method, Golf Club, La Vacherie, Mendoza, Argentina, 2010.

HEME AQUI integration through golf, Punta del Este, Uruguay, 2012.

Music as a means for studying, Golf Club, Mar del Plata, Argentina, 2013.

Training for Junior Sports Leaders, Buenos Aires, Argentina, 2011-2017.

Heme Aquí Here I am schools with the Goldfinger method

Argentina:

Palermo, CABA, 1999.

Tandil , Buenos Aires, 2006.

Villa Adelina, Buenos Aires, 2006.

Resistencia, Chaco, 2006.

Mar del Plata, Buenos Aires, 2007.

Necochea, Buenos Aires, 2008.

Pinamar, Buenos Aires, 2007.

San Luis, San Luis, 2007.

Monte Hermosos, Buenos Aires, 2008.

Bragado, Buenos Aires, 2008.

Berazategui, Buenos Aires, 2008.

Abroad:

Curitiba, Brazil, 2008.

Carmelo, Uruguay, 2008.

Colonia, Uruguay, 2009

Punta del Este, Uruguay, 2009.

Santiago de Chile, Chile, 2010.

Miami, USA, 2015.

AWARDS AND PRIZES GRANTED TO NORA LELCZUK

For her priceless dedication to integration of all sportsmen, granted by O.H. MACABI, 2003.

For her sense of transcendence in human values, granted by Existential and Psychological Center of Logotherapy, 2004.

For her worthy and noble work, granted by O. H. MACABI, 2004.

Monte Hermoso award, 2008.

Libertador award Mention for her work in education and integration, granted by Rotary Club Recoleta, 2011.

Genesis award, for her work in HEME AQUI as social innovator.

Remax award, for her ongoing work of social inclusion of people with special needs through golf, 2015.

Golf International meeting for people with mental disabilities, Maldonado Administration, Uruguay, 2015.

Ranelagh Golf Club Mention for her work for social inclusion of people with special needs, 2016.

Honorary Merit Diploma," Angeles que llaman ", for her support on inclusion, culture and principles, 2017.

Acknowledgment Diploma, Education Day I , Galeria de las Buenas Prácticas en Política, Management and innovative educational experiences, 2017.

Amazing women and their social and educational commitment Award, Beit Jana, 2018.

e-mail: noragoldfinger@gmail.com

www.hemeaqui.org